BACH'S FORTY-EIGHT PRELUDES AND FUGUES

ANALYSED FOR STUDENTS BY

FREDERICK ILIFFE

BOOK I

NOVELLO PUBLISHING LIMITED
8/9 Frith Street, London W1V 5TZ

Order No: NOV 630056

PREFACE.

WHAT Schumann said of J. S. Bach was certainly true: "Music owes almost as great a debt to him as a religion owes to its founder." Nowhere in the whole range of music is there a collection of pieces standing on a level with the Forty-eight Preludes and Fugues. The First Part of the work (Nos. I.—XXIV.) was completed by Bach in 1722, while he was at Cöthen, and the Second Part was put together at Leipzig, a little over a score of years later, about 1742-1744.* Very different from Handel, Bach rarely dated his works; but if reliable approximate data as regards the Second Part were not at hand, there is strong internal evidence that the pieces contained in it were written considerably later than those in the First Part. The aim and purpose of the "Forty-eight" may be summed up in a few words: (1) To prove that "Equal Temperament" was not only possible, but eminently desirable; (2) to provide a copious variety of pieces worthy of practice and study for Bach's pupils.

The object of the present Analysis§ is to place in the hands of students a detailed and exhaustive scheme of every Prelude and Fugue. In the Preludes the mode of procedure has been: (1) To give the Figure upon which each Prelude is built; (2) to give the Prelude itself in full and copiously marked, or in a reduced form showing the structure; (3) a "Summary" of the piece; and lastly, general "Remarks" upon the structure and treatment of the materials. For the Fugues a Tabulated Analysis—bar by bar—is first given, then a "Summary" and "Remarks" as before.

Admired as this work of Bach's is amongst musicians, it would appear that admiration has hitherto chiefly centred upon its Fugues, though the Preludes are quite as wonderful, and more unique, and the fineness of the work in many of them is of the highest possible order. A few words upon their characteristics may not be out of place, and at the same time it may not be unprofitable to divide them into groups, and to assign to such as represent different types of art their respective affinities. To those which owed their existence to Bach's extraordinary power of Preludizing, and his fondness for placing a graceful and ingenious superstructure on a carefully selected series of chords, would probably fall Nos. 1, 2, 5, 6, 11, 15, and 27. To those which originated from his innate love of Fugal and Imitative work, the following—Nos. 4, 7, 9, 12, 13, 14, 18, 19, 20, 23, 24, 25, 32, 34, 35, 37, 41, and 43. Those which may be said to fall under the head of a "Cantilena accompanied" would be Nos. 8, 10, and 16; while a solitary one (No. 17) was probably developed from the germ of a Dance movement.

Another consideration full of interest and importance, and closely connected with the above, is the manner in which structural principles or "Form" are illustrated in these Preludes. In Book I. we find Bach speculating or making independent and original experiments in structure, and working them out and

---

* It must not be supposed that the pieces contained in these Books were composed, or even put together at the precise dates mentioned above; on the contrary, their composition and compilation occupied a considerable time. Some of the Preludes in the First Book appeared also in a shortened form in some of the earlier editions (Forkel's Ed., 1801, Leipzig).

§ Made from the Bach Society's edition of this work.

perfecting them for himself, as in Nos. 8, 21, and 22. There is no direct influence of the Sonata type in the Preludes of this book; but in Book II. we find, together with original and beautiful experiments, such as Nos. 28, 46, 47, and 48, a goodly number of specimens of the old Sonata type, Nos. 33, 36, 39, and 42 being distinctly in this form; while the influence of the same mould is also, to a certain degree, stamped upon Nos. 26, 30, 31, 38, 40, and 44. Again, it is important to notice that two out of the above—Nos. 36 and 42—are, at the same time, prophetic of the splendour of the Modern Sonata form; while two others not yet mentioned—Nos. 29 and 45—are, with slight modifications, actually in this modern form as we know it to-day.

With regard to the Fugues—Bach's idea of a Fugue was far higher and nobler than that of any of his predecessors—of all forms it was the one he loved most, and in its sphere he reached the highest point of perfection attainable. With him a Fugue was a perfect organism, and to the study of its unfolding and development he gave the best efforts of his life, recognising at the outset the fact that a Fugue could not survive by the mere observance of formulas alone; for with him not only is device piled upon device, complexity upon complexity, ramification upon ramification, but the product is a composition teeming with real music. He revels in a strong flow of polyphony, and frequently also of elaborate interlacings of the parts, heedless if a passing note occasionally rubs somewhat roughly against the regular material, or if one accidental momentarily looks askance at another. It is nothing more than the many-sided pebbles in the rivulet which momentarily roll—and make music—against each other, as the stream proceeds along its determined course.

Enough has been outlined to show the intrinsic value of this wonderful collection, which has been subjected to the closest criticism by the best musicians for nearly a century, with the result that the more severe and searching the criticism, the more the beauties of the work unfold themselves; nor is it at all unlikely that when the present Sonata form—full of splendour though it is—shall have run its course, and shall have become a form of the past, thoughtful musicians will look for re-inspiration and guidance to many of these Preludes, the structure of which is peculiarly Bach's own. The suggestions offered by a patient study of a work of this stamp are almost innumerable; the fount is, so to say, inexhaustible, and the whole collection is securely placed upon the High Tower of Musical Art, the lasting joy and heritage of every earnest musician.

F. I.

DEFINITION OF FUGAL TERMS.

FUGUE.—A composition developed upon a certain Subject or theme, which is announced at first in one part only. This theme is imitated according to certain principles by the other parts composing the piece, which, as they " follow upon " or " fly after " the theme, give the distinctive title of *Fugue* (Latin, *fuga*) to this class of composition.

SUBJECT.— The theme upon which the composition is written. This theme should be (1) of a moderate length, so as to be retained without effort in the memory; (2) well defined in character, so as to be easily recognised at each appearance; (3) definite in tonality, so that there shall be no possibility of ambiguity as to its key. The Subject of a Fugue may be proposed in any part whatever.

ANSWER.—This is not a new theme, but a transposition of the Subject a fifth above (or a fourth below) by a different voice from that which announced the Subject.*

CODETTA.—" A connecting link." Some few notes used to connect the end of the Subject with the beginning of the Counter-subject. (For an excellent example see Fugue VII., bars $2^{(3)}\_3^{(1)}$.)

COUNTER-SUBJECT.—A supplemental melody to the Subject and Answer, written in double counterpoint. In the opening of a Fugue it is linked on to the end of the Subject by the aid of the Codetta and appears in the same part in which the Subject has just been enunciated. The Counter-subject is next to the Subject and Answer in point of importance.

EXPOSITION.—The opening section of the piece, in which all the voices make their first appearance by successively enunciating the Subject.

COUNTER-EXPOSITION.—A second exposition, in which the Subjects are mostly presented in reverse order. For example, in the Exposition, the Subject leads and the Answer follows, but in the Counter-exposition the Answer usually leads and the Subject follows. When all the parts are employed the Counter-exposition is said to be " complete," and "incomplete" should one or more parts be absent.

EPISODE.—A digressive section or phrase placed between two different blocks of thematic work. The modulatory passages in a well written Fugue are made by its Episodes, the materials of which are frequently taken from fragments of the Subject or Counter-subject.

STRETTO —(Latin, *stringo*=to draw close together). The bringing of the Subject and Answer nearer together than in the Exposition of the Fugue. Some Subjects are capable of stretto at various degrees of closeness, in this case the closest of all should be reserved for the last. [What is said above upon " complete " and " incomplete " Counter-expositions applies equally to the strettos.]

PEDAL.—A sustained bass note, generally the dominant or tonic, introduced near the end. Thematic imitations are effectively employed upon it.

CODA.—A few bars added to end up with. In fugal writing, the Coda generally consists of imitative work based upon the themes used during the course of the composition.

ABBREVIATIONS
TO DENOTE THE BARS UPON WHICH THE THEMES BEGIN AND END.

The small figures in brackets denote the beat, or fractions of the beat, of the bar to which reference is made.

$8^{(1)}$ means the 8th bar, first beat.

$8^{(-1)}$ means the 8th bar, last half the first beat. (In 4-4 time this will be the second quaver of the first beat.)

$8^{(½)}$ means the 8th bar, first half of the first beat. (In 4-4 time this will be the first quaver of the first beat.)

$8^{(¼)}$ means the 8th bar, first semiquaver of the first beat.

---

* Such an Answer as that just mentioned is called a " Real Answer"—*i.e.*, a real or exact transposition of the Subject. There are, however, many fugue subjects which, on account of the nature of our scales, demand a certain sacrifice in the melody of their Answers in order to preserve the requisite tonality, and these are called Tonal Answers.

PRELUDE I.

SUMMARY.

Bars 1—11, PERIOD I. (ending with Perfect Cadence in the key of the Dominant).

Bars 11—19, PERIOD II. (ending with Perfect Cadence in the key of the Tonic).

Bars 20—35, PERIOD III. (in reality a long Coda).

Bars 24—31, Dominant Pedal.

Bars 32—35, Tonic Pedal.

REMARKS.

This Prelude consists, mainly, of a simple series of chords, expressed by a constant reiteration of the following characteristic figure :—

which is repeated twice in every bar until the close, when it is expanded for variety into a freer and wider ranging Arpeggio.

The Harmony changes without exception at every bar.

Dignity and solidity are secured by the sostenuto figure in the Bass part.

The texture of the whole Prelude is homogeneous.

Its form is evidently an artistically matured version of a familiar type of extemporaneous preludizing by the use of a chain of chords.

PRELUDE I.

C MAJOR.

SHOWING THE STRUCTURE.

PERIOD I. C Major, establishing the key.

From here it moves away to the key of the Dominant.

PERIOD II. Modulates to gain colour.

Gently returns to Tonic.

PERIOD III. Coda.

Dominant Pedal.

Tonic Pedal.

* The bar frequently met with between 22 and 23 in the above, is generally agreed to have been an interpolation of Schwenke's. It is not found in any MS. except the one in his handwriting.

8251

FUGUE I. (C MAJOR)

IN FOUR PARTS.

Allegro moderato. ♪ = 120.

ANALYSIS.

ENUNCIATION SECTION.

Bars			KEYS.
1 (-1) — 2 (3)	Subject in Alto		C
2 (-3) — 4 (¾)	Real Answer in Treble		G
4 (-1) — 5 (3)	Answer in Tenor		G
5 (-3) — 7 (¾)	Subject in Bass		C
7 (-1) — 8 (3)	Subject in Treble		C
7 (-2) — 8 (4)	Answer in Tenor, in Stretto with the previous entry in Treble		G
9 (-1) — 10 (3)	Answer in Alto		G
10 (-3) — 12	Subject in Bass		G

MODULATORY SECTION.

Bars			KEYS.
10 (-4) — 12 (2)	Answer in Alto, in Stretto with the previous entry in the Bass.		G
12 (-1) — 13 (3)	Subject in Tenor. Full Close in A minor		A minor
14 (-1) — 15 (3)	Subject in Alto, resumed at once in C major		C
14 (-2) — 15 (2)	Answer (incomplete) in Tenor, in Stretto		C
15 (-1) — 16 (3)	Answer in Bass		G
15 (-3) — 16 (2)	Answer (incomplete) in Treble, concluding the first complete Stretto ...		G
16 (-2) — 17 (4)	Subject in Treble		C
16 (-3) — 18 (¾)	Answer in Alto		C
17 (-1) — 18 (3)	Answer in Tenor		D minor
17 (-3) — 19	Subject in Bass, concluding the second complete Stretto. Close in D ...		D minor
19 (-1) — 20 (3)	Subject in Tenor		D major
19 (-2) — 20 (4)	Answer in Alto, in Stretto		G
20 (-3) — 21 (2)	Subject in Bass (incomplete)		G
20 (-4) — 22 (2)	Answer in Treble, concluding the third complete Stretto		G

RECAPITULATORY SECTION.

Bars			KEYS.
21 (-3) — 23 (1)	Answer in Tenor, and Close in C major		C
24 (-1) — 25 (3)	Subject in Tenor on a Pedal C, which continues to the end of the Fugue		C
24 (-3) — 26 (1)	Answer in Alto, in Stretto		F
24 (-4) — 25 (2)	Answer (incomplete) in Treble		F
25 (3) — 27	Coda, built mainly on the concluding semiquaver figure of the Subject, and a figure derived from the ascending figure of the Opening		C

SUMMARY.

Exposition: Bars 1 — 6.	Stretti: Six.
Counter-exposition: Bars 7 — 10.	Tonic Pedal: Bars 24 — 27.
Episodes: None.	Coda: Bars 25 (3) — 27.

REMARKS.

(1.) This Fugue has a "real" Answer, and would be styled a "real" Fugue.

(2.) It has no Counter-subject.

(3.) The order in which the voices enter in the Exposition is unusual, as the Subject and Answer do not regularly alternate, but follow one another in the order: Subject, Answer, Answer, Subject.

(4.) In the Counter-exposition (bars 7 — 10) the voices enter in the same order as in the Exposition.

(5.) The Fugue has three complete and three incomplete Stretti. The Stretti at bar 7, at bar 10, and at bars 24 — 25 are incomplete, because all the voices do not take part in them. The complete Stretti in which all the voices take part are in bars 14 — 15, 16 — 18, and 19 — 21

PRELUDE II.

SUMMARY.

Bars 1—14, PERIOD I. (ending in the Relative Major).

Bars 14—28, PERIOD II. (ending on the Dominant).

Bars 28—38, PERIOD III. (built upon the Dominant and Tonic Pedals).

Bars 1—6, Tonic Pedal.

Bars 28—33, Dominant Pedal.

Bars 34—38, Tonic Pedal.

REMARKS.

This Prelude is constructed on chords of a simple nature, which underlie the constant reiteration of the following figure :—

This figure, which is persistent throughout the Prelude, till five bars from the end, takes its distinctive character from the Passing note, which almost always forms the third note in each group of four.

In Period I. there is a Sectional division at bar 4 ([1]), and in Period II. at bar 18 ([1]).

In Period III. there is no division in the strict sense of the word, though there are differences of "tempo" at bars 34 and 35.

The artistic method of this Prelude is akin to that of the first, though much more animated and energetic, owing to the use of the dissonant passing notes in each characteristic figure.

PRELUDE II.

C MINOR.

SHOWING THE STRUCTURE.

Allegro con brio. ♩ = 120.

PERIOD I. C Minor, establishing the key. From here it moves by degrees away from the original key to its Relative Major (E♭). PERIOD II. Moving gently back to C Minor, moves to Dominant Pedal, and further clenches the original key.
Dominant Pedal.

Presto. ♩ = 132.

PERIOD III.

(Flourish.)

Allegro.

FUGUE II. (C MINOR).

IN THREE PARTS.

Allegro ma non troppo. ♩ = 88.

(*p*)

ANALYSIS.

ENUNCIATION SECTION.

			KEYS.
Bars 1 (-1) — 3 (¼)	Subject in Alto		C minor
„ 3 (-1) — 5 (¾)	Tonal Answer in Treble, with Counter-subject in Alto		G minor
„ 5 — 7	Codetta formed from the first limb of the Subject in the Treble, and from the first few notes of the Counter-subject in contrary motion in the Alto, both moving in an ascending sequence. It modulates from G minor to C minor.		
„ 7 (-1) — 9 (¼)	Subject in Bass. Counter-subject in Treble		C minor

MODULATORY SECTION.

„ 9 (-1) — 11 (1)	Episode I., modulating from C minor to E♭ major.		
„ 11 (-1) — 13 (¼)	Subject in Treble. Counter-subject in Bass		E♭ major
„ 13 (-1) — 15 (⅛)	Episode II., modulating from E♭ major to C minor.		
„ 15 (-1) — 17 (½)	Answer in Alto. Counter-subject in Treble		G minor
„ 17 (-1) — 20 (½)	Episode III., modulating from G minor to C minor.		
„ 20 (-1) — 22 (¼)	Subject in Treble. Counter-subject in Alto		C minor
„ 22 — 26 (3)	Episode IV., modulating from C minor to E♭ major and back to C minor.		

RECAPITULATORY SECTION.

„ 26 (3) — 28 (3)	Subject in Bass. Counter-subject divided between the Treble and Alto...		C minor
„ 29 (3) — 31	Tonic Pedal and Coda		C minor
„ 29 (-3) — 31	Subject in Treble. Counter-subject absent, the inner parts being independent. Final chord major, called Tierce de Picardie...		C major

SUMMARY.

Exposition : Bars 1 — 9.	Episodes : Four.
Counter-exposition : None.	Stretti : None.
Codetta : One (bars 5 — 6).	Coda, Tonic Pedal : Bars 29 (3) — 31.

REMARKS.

(1.) This Fugue has a "tonal" Answer, and would be styled a "tonal" Fugue. The fourth note of the Answer is altered for the sake of tonality.

(2.) It has a Counter-subject. This is constructed according to the rules of Double Counterpoint in the octave, so that when used above, and when used below the Subject and Answer, it may produce good harmony.

(3.) The material upon which the four Episodes are constructed is as follows :—

Episode I. is constructed from the first limb of the Subject in the Treble and Alto, the latter imitating the Treble at the 5th below. The running Bass part is built upon the first limb of the Counter-subject. All three parts move in a descending sequence.

Episode II. The Treble has a running Counterpoint formed from the first limb of the Counter-subject taken here in an ascending direction. The two underparts (formed from the quaver portion of the same) move in 3rds with each other.

Episode III. The Bass is formed from the first limb of the Subject, the Alto from the first limb of the Counter-subject taken in an ascending direction, the Treble having a detached figure.

Episode IV. The Treble and Alto are formed from the first limb of the Subject, the latter imitating the Treble at the 5th below, the running Bass part being taken from the first limb of the Counter-subject. All three parts move in a descending sequence. (Compare Episode I.)

PRELUDE III.

SUMMARY.

Bars 1—31, PERIOD I. (ending in the Relative Minor).
Bars 31(^{8})—55, PERIOD II. (Modulatory).
Bars 55—104, PERIOD III. (Repetition of Opening Subject and Coda).

Bars 63—73 (Dominant Pedal).
Bars 87—102 (Dominant Pedal).
Bars 63—104 (Coda).

REMARKS.

This Prelude is built upon the following figures :—

Period I. contains four Phrases. The figure which appears in the Treble in Phrases I. and III. is assigned to the Bass in Phrases II. and IV., and the figure which appears in the Bass in Phrases I. and III. is assigned to the Treble in Phrases II. and IV.

Period II. is Modulatory until bar 47, when the Theme occurs in the Subdominant. PERIOD III. begins with the repetition of the Opening Subject. Bars 63—74, and bars 87—96 contain a melodic figure, employed in couplets, *i.e.*, two bars are allotted to each feature.

Period III. as it proceeds is "fined down" more and more until the conclusion, by the additional employment of the Dominant Pedals and Coda.

This Prelude is a remarkable instance of what it is possible to do upon the same root principles of procedure as the Modern Sonata, but on totally different lines. From bars 1—31 the 1st Theme is used four times in different keys. In the Modulatory portion an entirely new Theme is started. The unusual length of the Coda is also very notable.

PRELUDE III.

C♯ MAJOR.

SHOWING THE FRAMEWORK, MELODIC FEATURES, AND PHRASING.

Allegro vivace. ♩• = 88.

PERIOD I. C♯ Major, establishing the key.

Th. in the Dominant.

Th. in the Supertonic.

Th. in the Relative Minor.

8251.

(7)

PRELUDE III.

PERIOD II. (Modulatory) starting from A♯ Minor and touching upon the keys of E♯, D♯, and G♯ Minors, and working

Th. in the Subdominant.

on for contrast to the key of the Subdominant.

PERIOD III. Repetition of Opening Theme in original key.

CODA.

Dominant Pedal.

(Sequence of bars

75—79 a tone lower.)

Dominant Pedal.

FUGUE III. (C♯ MAJOR).

IN THREE PARTS.

Allegro grazioso. ♩ = 120.

ANALYSIS.

ENUNCIATION SECTION.

Bars			KEYS.
Bars	1 (-2) — 3 (½)	Subject in Treble	C♯
"	3 (-2) — 5 (½)	Tonal Answer in Alto, with Counter-subject I. in Treble	G♯
"	5 (-2) — 7 (½)	Subject in Bass, with Counter-subject II. in Treble and Counter-subject I. in Alto	C♯
"	7 (-1) — 10 (2)	Episode I., modulating from C♯ major to G♯ major by descending sequence. (The Counter-subject II. at its conclusion overlaps the commencement of this Episode.)	
"	10 (-2) — 12 (½)	Answer in Treble, Counter-subject in Alto, Counter-subject III. in Bass. (This latter melody is not used again until bars 51 (-3) — 53 (3))...	G♯

MODULATORY SECTION.

"	12 (-1) — 14	Episode II., modulating from G♯ major to D♯ minor. (Compare this with Episode I. and notice the rolling semiquaver figure in the Bass now given to the Treble.)	
"	14 (-2) — 16 (½)	Subject in Bass, Counter-subject I. in Treble, Alto silent	A♯ minor
"	16 — 19	Episode III., modulating from A♯ minor to E♯ minor. Materials the same as previous Episodes, differently disposed.	
"	19 (-2) — 21 (½)	Answer in Alto, Counter-subject I. in Bass, Counter-subject II. in Treble	E♯ minor
"	21 — 22	Codetta in all three parts, and close in E♯ minor.	
"	22 (-3) — 24	Episode IV., modulating from E♯ minor to G♯ major.	
"	24 (-4) — 26 (3)	Answer in Treble	G♯
"	25 — 26 (3)	Counter-subject I. in Bass, Counter-subject II. in Alto.	
"	26 (-4) — 28 (3)	Subject in Alto, with Counter-subject II. in Bass, and Counter-subject I. in Treble	C♯
"	28 (-3) — 42	Episode V., modulating from C♯ major, through A♯ minor, F♯ major, D♯ minor, F♯ major, and back to C♯, by sequences; with frequent allusions to fragments of Subject.	

RECAPITULATORY SECTION.

"	42 (-2) — 44 (½)	Subject in Treble, with Counter-subject I. in Bass	C♯
"	44 (-2) — 46 (½)	Answer in Alto, Counter-subject I. in Treble, Counter-subject II. in Bass	G♯
"	46 (-2) — 48 (½)	Subject in Bass, Counter-subject I. in Alto, Counter-subject II. in Treble	C♯
"	48 — 51 (4)	Episode VI., modulating from C♯ major, through F♯ major, D♯ minor, G♯ minor, and back to C♯.	
"	51 (-3) — 53 (3)	Counter-subject III. in Bass.	
"	51 (-4) — 53 (3)	Subject in Treble, with Counter-subject I. in Alto, and Counter-subject III. in Bass	C♯
"	53 (3) — 55	Coda, comprising a free version of Subject in Treble	C♯

SUMMARY.

Exposition: Bars 1 — 7.
Counter-exposition: None.
Codetta: One (bar 21).

Episodes: Six.
Stretti: None.
Coda: Bars 53 — 55.

REMARKS.

(1.) This Fugue has a Tonal Answer, and would be styled a Tonal Fugue. The alteration in the Answer, for the sake of tonality, is made from the first note to the second.

(2.) The first Counter-subject is used regularly throughout the Fugue, but the second Counter-subject is absent on four occasions—(1) at bar 10, (2) at bar 14, (3) at bar 42, and (4) at bar 52

(3.) It has no Counter-exposition, the Answer in bar 10 being merely redundant, in order to show the Counter-subject below it.

(4.) The construction of the Episodes is as follows:—

Episode I. (bar 7). The Treble proposes a new subject, which is imitated freely by the Alto, the Bass having a running Counterpoint. All three parts move in a descending sequence.

Episode II. (bar 12). A detached figure (formed from the Treble of Episode I.) is proposed by the Bass, imitated freely by the Tenor; the rolling figure, which in the former Episode was entrusted to the Bass, is here assigned to the Treble.

Episode III. (bar 16). A figure (first noticeable in bar $9^{(3)}$) is proposed by the Treble, imitated by the Alto; the rolling figure in the Bass being a transposition of that in Episode I.

Episode IV. (bar 22). The first part of this (bars 21———$22^{(3)}$) is joined to the previous Thematic work, which it carries on to a perfect cadence in E$\sharp$ minor. The second part consists of an imitation of the first limb of the Subject in the Treble in a descending sequence, the Tenor having a running Counterpoint.

Episode V. (bar 28). This is the most important: its first section, as far as bar $30^{(3)}$, should be compared with Episode I.; its second section, to bar $34^{(3)}$, transposes the melodic figures of the former to different parts. From bar 35 to 42 two parts only are employed, interchanging sequentially fragments of the Subject with each other.

Episode VI. (bar 48). This is a summary of the figures used in the preceding Episodes, with the momentary addition of a new figure in the Treble and Alto (bar 48).

(5.) This Fugue is remarkable for its employment of two Counter-subjects, and also—though on two occasions only—of a third Counter-subject. Also for the number of its Episodes and their great importance in the scheme of the work.

PRELUDE IV.

SUMMARY.

This Prelude is built upon the following figure :—

Bars 1—14, PERIOD I. (ending in the Dominant Minor, G♯).
Bars 14 (⁶)—39, PERIOD II. (mostly in the original key).

REMARKS.

Period I. may be divided into three Sections, the first division being at bar 4, where the Dominant is reached ; the second at bar 8, where Theme I. appears in the Tenor in the Relative Major, and the third at bar 14, where there is a Perfect Cadence in the Dominant Minor.

Periods I. and II. are both Imitative. At the opening of Period I. the Tenor imitates the Treble at the distance of one bar. In bar 5, a second Theme appears in the Treble, which is repeated in the two following bars in a descending Sequence. In Period II. both Themes are used for development, after bar 23, however, Theme II. disappears, and the piece is worked with material drawn from Theme I., the Bass part freely imitating the Treble.

A remarkable example of interest being maintained without Modulation. Almost the whole Prelude centralises on C♯, and variety is obtained by changes in the manner of the treatment of the ideas, rather than by tonal contrast.

PRELUDE IV.

C♯ MINOR.

SHOWING THE STRUCTURE.

Th. II
Period II.
Imitation of Th. I.
Th. II. slightly elaborated.
B Major.
Fragment of Th. I.
C♯ Minor.
Th. II.
Th. I.
Descending Sequence.
All in the original key (C♯ Minor), variety being secured by changes in the mode of treatment of ideas.
From this point the Bass freely imitates the Treble.
Imitation of Th. I.
Passage strengthening the Dominant of C♯ Minor.
Fragment of Th. II.
Imitation of Th. I.
Working gradually back to Tonic.
Imitation of Th. I.

FUGUE IV. (C♯ MINOR).

IN FIVE PARTS.

ANALYSIS.

ENUNCIATION SECTION.

			KEYS.
Bars	1 ____ 4 (1)	Subject in Bass	C♯ minor
"	4 ____ 7 (2)	Real Answer in Tenor	G♯ minor
"	7 (3) __10 (2)	Subject in Alto	C♯ minor
"	11 ____ 12	Codetta.	
"	12 (3) __14 (3)	Answer in Second Treble. Compare this with the previous Answer in Tenor. It is to be noted that except its first note it is in F♯ minor instead of G♯ minor.	
"	14 (3) __17	Subject in First Treble	C♯ minor
"	18 ____ 19	Codetta.	
"	19 (3) __22 (1)	Answer in Tenor	G♯ minor
"	22 (4) __25	Subject in Tenor	F♯ minor
"	25 (3) __29	Answer in Alto	C♯ minor

MODULATORY SECTION.

"	29 (3) __32	Answer in Bass	B major
"	32 (3) __35	Subject in Alto	E major
"	35 (2) __38	Counter-subject I. in First Treble (this being its first appearance).	
"	35 (3) __38 (2)	Subject in Tenor	C♯ minor
"	38 (3) __41 (4)	Answer in Alto. Counter-subject I. in First Treble	G♯ minor
"	41 ____ 44	Episode I., modulating from G♯ minor to C♯ minor. The Tenor is an inversion of the Counter-subject of the Treble in an ascending sequence.	
"	44 (3) __47 (3)	Subject in Second Treble. Counter-subject I. in Bass	C♯ minor
"	46 (2) __48 (4)	Counter-subject I. in First Treble.	
"	49 ____ 51	Subject in First Treble. Counter-subject I. in Second Treble. Counter-subject II. in Tenor, this being the first appearance of the latter ...	F♯ minor
"	51 (3) __54	Subject in Bass. Counter-subject I. in Tenor	F♯ minor
"	52 (2) __54	Counter-subject II. in First Treble.	
"	54 (3) __57	Answer in Second Treble. Counter-subject I. in Tenor	A major
"	55 (2) __57	Counter-subject II. in Bass.	
"	57 ____ 59	Counter-subject I. in First Treble. Counter-subject II. in Second Treble.	
"	59 ____ 62	Subject in First Treble. Counter-subject I. in Second Treble	C♯ minor
"	60 (2) __62	Counter-subject II. in Alto.	
"	62 (2) __65	Episode II., modulating from C♯ minor to G♯ major. Counter-subject II. in First Treble. Counter-subject I. in Second Treble.	
"	64 (2) __66	Counter-subject II. in Tenor.	
"	65 ____ 66 (3)	Counter-subject II. in Bass.	
"	66 ____ 68	Subject in First Treble. Counter-subject I. in Bass	D♯ minor
"	67 (2) __69 (3)	Counter-subject II. in Second Treble.	
"	69 ____ 71	Counter-subject I. in First Soprano. Counter-subject II. in Tenor.	
"	71 (2) __73	Counter-subject II. in Second Treble.	
"	73 ____ 76 (1)	Subject in Bass. Counter-subject I. in Alto	C♯ minor
"	74 (2) __76	Counter-subject II. in Tenor.	
"	76 ____ 79	Subject in First Treble. Counter-subject I. in Bass	C♯ minor
"	77 ____ 78 (3)	Counter-subject II. in Second Treble.	
"	78 (3) __81	Counter-subject I. in Second Treble.	
"	79 (2) __81	Counter-subject II. in Bass.	

FUGUE IV.

MODULATORY SECTION—*continued.*

		KEYS.
Bars 81____84	Subject in Tenor. Counter-subject I. in First Treble	C♯ minor
,, 82 (2)____84	Counter-subject II. in Alto.	
,, 84____86	Episode III., modulating from C♯ minor to F♯ minor. Counter-subject I. in First Treble. Counter-subject II. in Tenor.	
,, 85 (2)____87	Counter-subject II. in Second Treble	F♯ minor
,, 86____88	Counter-subject I. in First Treble. Counter-subject II. in Bass.	
,, 89____92 (1)	Subject in First Treble	C♯ minor
,, 90____92	Counter-subject II. in Bass.	
,, 92____94 (1)	Counter-subject I. in Tenor. Counter-subject II. in First Treble.	
,, 93 (2)____95 (2)	Counter-subject II. in Second Treble.	
,, 94____96	Subject in First Treble. Counter-subject II. in Tenor	E major
,, 95 (2)____97	Counter-subject II. in Alto. Answer in Second Treble	B major
,, 96____98	Counter-subject II. in Tenor. Subject in First Treble	F♯ minor

RECAPITULATORY SECTION.

		KEYS.
,, 97____100	Answer in Bass. Counter-subject II. in Alto	C♯ minor
,, 98____100	Counter-subject II. in Second Treble, in Tenor, in First Treble, successively in Stretto.	
,, 100____102 (2)	Codetta. Subject in Tenor. Counter-subject II. in Bass	C♯ minor
,, 102____104	Counter-subject II. in Tenor.	
,, 103 (2)____104 (3)	Counter-subject II. in Alto.	
,, 104____106 (1)	Counter-subject II. in Second Treble.	
,, 105 (2)____106 (3)	Counter-subject II. in Tenor, on Dominant Pedal.	
,, 107 (2)____108 (3)	Subject in First Treble. Counter-subject II. in Second Treble and Alto, in thirds simultaneously	C♯ minor
,, 108 (2) _109 (4)	Counter-subject II. in Tenor.	
,, 110____115	Coda	C♯ minor
,, 112____115	Tonic Pedal	C♯
,, 112 (3)____115	Imitation of Subject in Second Treble	C♯ major
,, 113 (2)____115	Counter-subject II. in Alto. Final Chord major. Tierce de Picardie ...	C♯ major

SUMMARY.

Exposition : Bars 1____17.

Counter-exposition (incomplete) : Bars 19____29.

Codettas : Two.

Episodes : Three.

Stretti : Several examples between bars 92____108 in which the Subject, Answer, and Counter-subject II. exclusively take part.

Coda : Bars 110____115.

Dominant Pedal : Bars 105____108.

Tonic Pedal : Bars 112____115.

REMARKS.

(1.) This Fugue is in five parts. It has a "real" Answer and would be styled a "real" Fugue.

(2.) The Exposition is remarkable for the firmness and solidity with which it is built up. Neither of the Counter-subjects appear in it, but in their place another melody is used, which, however, disappears after bar 40.

(3.) The Counter-exposition is not regularly worked and is incomplete (bars 19____29). The entries of the Subject and Answer also do not appear in regular order.

(4.) The Counter-subjects make their appearance somewhat late, the Counter-subject I. appearing first in bar 35 and the Counter-subject II. in bar 49.

(5.) The second Counter-subject is employed much more frequently than the first; indeed, after bar 94 the Counter-subject I. disappears, but the Counter-subject II. after this point is used sixteen times.

(6.) Triple Counterpoint is chiefly used in this Fugue, as there are two Counter-subjects to be worked above and below the Subject and Answer.

(7.) The device of Inversion of the first Counter-subject is used in bars 41____43 in an ascending sequence. There is no Augmentation or Diminution proper.

(8.) Great prominence is given to Counter-subject II. in the latter part of the Fugue, from bar 93 to the end.

PRELUDE V.

SUMMARY.

This Prelude is an example of the expansion of the simpler method of Arpeggios (as seen in Nos. 1 and 2) into more definitely vivid figures, occupying a proportionately wider range of the key-board. It is founded upon the following figure : —

Bars 1—13, PERIOD I. (ending with Perfect Cadence in the Tonic).

Bars 13—20, PERIOD II. (ending with Perfect Cadence in the Subdominant).

Bars 20—25, PERIOD III. (Episodal, ending with Perfect Cadence in the Tonic).

Bars 25—35, PERIOD IV. (Coda, comprising Dominant Pedal in bars 27—30).

REMARKS.

In the structure of the Bass and Treble, the former, after establishing its chord, frequently skips through part of its Arpeggio and to its Octave; the Treble is made up of the component parts of the various chords employed, interspersed with Passing Notes.

Bars 6 and 7 are an Imitation of bars 3 and 4 in the fourth below.

Bars 20—25 are a recapitulation in the Subdominant of the opening bars.

PERIOD I. may be divided into two Sections at bar 6 (¹).

PERIODS II. and III. cannot be subdivided.

PRELUDE V.

D MAJOR.

SHOWING THE MELODIC FEATURES. THE BASS PART DRAWN OUT IN LONG NOTES TO SHOW THE GROUNDWORK.

PERIOD I. D Major, establishing the key. {From here it moves to the Dominant, and confirms it by a Perfect Cadence.} {From here it modulates transiently to E Minor,}

B Minor, F♯ Minor, B Major, {E Minor, and back to D, clenching the Tonic by a Perfect Cadence.} PERIOD II. Gradually moving to

A Minor, E Minor, B Minor, {A Minor, then to the Subdominant G.} {PERIOD III. (Episodal.) Transposition of opening

bars into the Subdominant. Return to the Tonic. PERIOD IV. (Coda.) Dominant Pedal.

(Bravura passage.)

8251.

(16)

FUGUE V. (D MAJOR).

IN FOUR PARTS.

Allegro maestoso. ♩ = 76.

(*f resoluto.*)

ANALYSIS.

ENUNCIATION SECTION.

Bars			KEYS.
1 (2) — 2 (1)	Subject in Bass		D
" 2 (2) — 3 (1)	Real Answer in Tenor		A
" 3 — 4 (1)	Codetta.		
" 4 (2) — 5 (1)	Subject in Alto		D
" 5 (2) — 6	Answer in Treble		A
" 6 — 7	Codetta, containing allusions to the first figure of Subject.		
" 7 (2) — 8	Subject in Bass		D

MODULATORY SECTION.

" 8 ( ) — 9	Answer in Treble		B minor
" 9 (2) — 11 (1)	Episode I., modulating from B minor to G major, introducing new features of importance.		
" 11 (2) — 12	Subject in Treble		G
" 12 (2) — 13	Answer in Alto		D
" 13 (2) — 14	Answer (incomplete) in Bass		D
" 14 (2) — 15 (1)	Subject in Tenor		G
" 15 (2) — 16	Answer in Bass and Close in E minor		E minor
" 17 — 19	Episode II., modulating from E minor to G major, the material the same as in Episode I.		
" 20 — 22	Free imitations of the first limb of the Subject.		

RECAPITULATORY SECTION.

" 23 — 27	Close in D and Coda, founded on figures of Subject		D

SUMMARY.

Exposition : Bars 1 — 6.
Counter-exposition : None.
Counter-subject : None.
Episodes : Two.
Stretti : None.
Pedal : None.

REMARKS.

(1.) This Fugue has a " real " Answer, and would be styled a " real " Fugue.

(2.) In Episode I. a new melodic figure is introduced in the Treble, the Alto and Tenor being made up of the second limb of the Subject, while the Bass is formed from its first group of demisemiquavers.

In Episode II. the melodic figures employed in the Treble and Bass of Episode I. are reversed.

(3.) There are no devices of Augmentation, Diminution, or Inversion employed, yet owing to the strongly characteristic nature of the first limb of the Subject this is a very interesting and closely knit— though somewhat irregular—Fugue.

PRELUDE VI.

SUMMARY.

This Prelude is founded upon the following figure:—

Bars 1—6, Period I. (ending with Perfect Cadence in the Relative Major, **F**).

Bars 6—15, Period II. (ending with the Perfect Cadence in the Tonic Major, **D**).

Bars 15—26, Period III. (Coda).

Bars 1—2 (^{2}), Tonic Pedal.

Bars 15—21 (^{2}), Tonic Pedal.

Bar 23, Dominant Pedal.

REMARKS.

In the early part of this Prelude the sequential character of some of its Phrases should be noted, for instance, bars 6 (^{2})—8 (^{1}) are imitated by bars 8 (^{2})—10 (^{1}) in an ascending Sequence. It is then broken for two bars, but re-appears in bars 12 (^{2})—14.

Period II. is Modulatory; its first Phrase, bars 6 (^{2})—8 (^{1}), modulating to G Minor (Subdominant), its second Phrase to A Minor (Dominant), and so on, proceeding finally to the Tonic Major (bar 15), where the Coda is commenced.

PRELUDE VI.

D MINOR.

SHOWING THE STRUCTURE.

Allegro ma non troppo. ♩ = 80.

PERIOD I. D Minor, establishing the key.   From here it gently moves away for contrast to the Relative Major.

Tonic Pedal.

PERIOD II. Proposition of material for Sequence.   Sequence of bars 6 — 8.

Imitation of former Sequence.

PERIOD III.
(Coda.)

Tonic Pedal.

FUGUE VI. (D minor).

IN THREE PARTS.

ANALYSIS.

Enunciation Section.

				KEYS
Bars	1 (-1) __ 3 (1)	Subject in Treble		D
"	3 (-1) __ 5 (1)	Real Answer in Alto, with Counter-subject in Treble		A
"	5 __ 6	Codetta, founded on Counter-subject.		
"	6 (-1) __ 8 (1)	Subject in Bass. First limb of Counter-subject in Treble		D
"	7 (-1) __ 8 (1)	Second limb of Counter-subject in Alto.		

Modulatory Section.

				KEYS
"	8 (-1) __ 10 (1)	Subject (irregular as to position) in Treble. Counter-subject in Bass ...		D
"	10 __ 13	Episode I., modulating from D to A, forming a descending sequence.		
"	12 __ 13 (1)	Subject (fragment of) in Bass, the first note being altered (E♭ instead of F). Answer in Alto (first five notes only) by Inversion		D
"	13 (1) __ 15	Subject in Treble. Counter-subject (first part only) in Bass		A
"	13 (-1) __ 16	Stretto I. (incomplete).		
"	14 (-1) __ 16	Answer by Inversion in Alto. Ascending sequential figure in the Bass in bars 15 and 16		A
"	17 __ 20	Fragment of Counter-subject in Treble. Subject in Bass and Subject in Alto successively, in Stretto. Close in A in bar 21		A A
"	21 __ 23 (⅔)	Subject in Bass. Counter-subject in Treble		A A
"	22 (-1) __ 24	Answer by Inversion in Treble. Stretto III. (incomplete)		A D
"	23 (-1) __ 25	Subject by Inversion in Bass		D
"	24 __ 25	Counter-subject in Treble.		
"	25 __ 27	Episode II., modulating from D minor to G minor.		
"	26 __ 27	Subject by Inversion in Bass		G
"	27 (-1) __ 29 (2)	Answer by Inversion in Treble. Stretto IV. (complete)		A
"	28 __ 30 (1)	Subject in Alto.		
"	29 __ 31 (1)	Answer by Inversion in Bass, passing to G minor		D
"	31 __ 33	Episode III., modulating from G minor to D minor by way of F.		
"	33 (-1) __ 34	Subject in Alto (incomplete)		D
"	34 (-1) __ 36	Subject in Bass. Stretto V. (incomplete)		D
"	36 __ 39	Episode IV., modulating from G minor to D minor.		

Recapitulatory Section.

				KEYS
"	39 (-1) __ 41	Subject in Bass		D
"	40 __ 42	Subject in Alto. Stretto VI. (incomplete)		D
"	42 __ 44	Coda		D
"	43 __ 44	Pedal. Final chord major. Tierce de Picardie.		

FUGUE VI.

SUMMARY.

Exposition: Bars 1——8.

Counter-exposition: None.

Episodes: Four.

Stretti: Six, one being complete and five incomplete. The entries are all exactly at one bar's distance from each other.

Free Inversion of the Subject and Answer: Several instances.

Coda: Bars 42——44.

Tonic Pedal: Bars 43——44.

REMARKS.

(1.) This Fugue has a "real" Answer, and would be called a "real" Fugue.

(2.) The treatment of the Subject is remarkable on account of its frequent employment of the major instead of the minor third. After the Exposition the theme is used no less than eight times with the major third.

(3.) This Fugue contains the device of Inversion of the Subject and Answer.

(4.) At bar 7 (·¹) the Counter-subject is transferred from the Treble to the Alto, half way through.

(5.) The Episodes are constructed from material taken from the Counter-subject.

(6.) On the Tonic Pedal, the Subject is used in the second and third voices by inversion, and at the same time by direct motion in the fourth and fifth voices (bar 43), forming a succession of rich harmonies in six parts, for the conclusion.

PRELUDE VII.

SUMMARY.

Bars 1—10, PERIOD I. (concise statement of Theme I, and confirmation of key of Tonic).

Bars 10—25, PERIOD II. (ending on the Dominant).

Bars 25—35, PERIOD III. (mostly in B♭, and ending on the Mediant Minor, G).

Bars 35—41 ([8]), PERIOD IV. (ending on the Relative Minor, C).

Bars 41—58 ([8]), PERIOD V. (ending on the Subdominant Major, A♭).

Bars 58 ([4])—70, PERIOD VI. (ending on the Tonic).

Bars 1—4, Tonic Pedal.

Bars 8—10 ([1]), Dominant Pedal.

Bars 68—70, Tonic Pedal and Coda.

REMARKS.

Bars 1—10 are devoted to establishing the key of the Tonic (E♭), and presenting Theme I. in its most concise form. Bars 10—25 introduce Theme II. in a closely linked chain of suspensions induced by Imitations. At Bar 25 Theme I. is resumed in an extended form and combined with Theme II., this latter being written in Double Counterpoint in the Octave and Twelfth* with Theme I. The remainder of the Prelude is devoted to an almost ceaseless interlacing of the two Themes.

PRELUDE VII.
E♭ MAJOR.
SHOWING THE STRUCTURE.

---

* Instances of its employment in Double Counterpoint in the Twelfth occur at bars 47 ([1])—49 ([8]) and 68 ([1]).

PRELUDE VII.

PRELUDE VII.

52
53
54
Th. II.
Th. I.
Th. II.
55
56
57
Th. II.
Th. I.
58
Th. II.
59
60
Period VI.
61
Th. I.
62
63
Th. II.
64
65
Th. II.
66
Th. II.
Fragment of Th. I.
67
68
69
70
Th. I.
Th. II.
Fragment of Th. I

FUGUE VII. (E♭ MAJOR)

IN THREE PARTS.

Allegro con brio. ♩ = 108.

ANALYSIS.

ENUNCIATION SECTION.

Bars			KEYS
Bars 1———2 (3)	Subject in Treble, ending on the first semiquaver of beat 3, bar 2; the remaining semiquavers in the Treble, including the first quaver of bar 3, forming a short Codetta, the figure of which becomes very prominent in the course of the Fugue		E♭ & B♭ *
" 3———4 (3)	Tonal Answer in Alto, with Counter-subject in Treble		B♭ & E♭
" 4 (-3)——6	Codetta, founded mainly on the figure of the first Codetta.		
" 6———7 (3)	Subject in Bass. Counter-subject in Alto		E♭ & B♭
" 7 (3)——11	Episode I., modulating from B♭ to E♭, formed from the figure used in the first Codetta.		
" 11———12 (3)	Answer in Treble. Counter-subject in Bass		E♭

MODULATORY SECTION.

" 12 (-3)——17 (3)	Episode II., modulating from E♭ major to C minor by sequence.		
" 17 (3)——19 (1)	Close in C minor. Answer in Alto. Counter-subject in Treble... ...		C minor
" 19———20 (3)	Codetta.		C minor &
" 20 (3)——22 (1)	Subject in Bass. Counter-subject in Alto		G minor
" 22———26	Episode III., modulating from G minor to E♭ major.		
" 26———27 (3)	Answer in Bass. Counter-subject in Treble		E♭
" 27 (3)——29	Episode IV., modulating from E♭, through B♭ and back to E♭.		
" 29———30 (3)	Subject in Treble. Counter-subject in Alto		E♭ & B♭
" 30 (-3)——34	Episode V., modulating from E♭, through A♭ and B♭, back to E♭.		

RECAPITULATORY SECTION.

" 34———35 (3)	Answer in Alto. Counter-Subject absent		E♭
" 35———37	Coda		E♭

SUMMARY.

Exposition : Bars 1———7.	Episodes : Five.
Counter-exposition : None.	Stretti : None.
Codettas : Three.	Coda : Bars 35———37.

REMARKS.

(1.) This Fugue has a " tonal " Answer, and would be styled a " tonal " Fugue. The alteration in the Answer, for the sake of tonality, is made from the first note to the second.

(2.) An excellent example of the use and importance of the Codetta is shown in bar 2.

(3.) The Episodes are formed from the material employed in the first Codetta. In Episode V. two points should be specially noticed, (1) the strides of the 9th in the melodic figure of the Treble, (2) the free imitation by the Alto in contrary motion of the Arpeggio figure of the Bass.

(4.) In the Coda the Bass momentarily imitates the descending figure of the Treble.

* The second limb of the Subject is distinctly in the key of B♭.

PRELUDE VIII.

SUMMARY.

The impassioned Cantilena is supported by the characteristic repetition of the Chord, three times in each bar :—

Bars 1—16 (¹), PERIOD I. (ending with Perfect Cadence in the key of the Dominant Minor, B♭).
Bars 16—28, PERIOD II. (Modulatory).
Bars 28—40, PERIOD III. (Coda).

REMARKS.

Period I. may be divided into four Phrases; the first Phrase ending in the Tonic at bar 4; the second in the Subdominant Minor (A♭) at bar 8; the third in the Dominant Minor (B♭) at bar 12; and the fourth in the Dominant Minor by a Perfect Cadence at bar 16.

Period II. has two divisions (1) in bar 20, (2) in bar 28, where the Coda is reached. This Period aims at continuity rather than subdivision.

Note the striking pair of Interrupted Cadences, bars **28** and **37**, successively deferring the close of the movement consistently with the pathetic mood of the Music.

PRELUDE VIII.

E♭ MINOR.

SHOWING THE STRUCTURE.

PRELUDE VIII.

to the Dominant Minor.

Marked procedure by Perfect Cadence

to the Dominant Minor. PERIOD II. (Modulatory).

Imitation of the Treble at the Octave.

Free Imitation of figure

used in bar 20. Return to the Original key (E♭ Minor). CODA. PERIOD III. Gently moving to Subdominant.

Gradual return to E♭, and confirmation of the key.
(Bravura passage.)

FUGUE VIII. (D♯ MINOR).

IN THREE PARTS.

Andante con moto. ♩ = 76.

(legato.)

ANALYSIS.

ENUNCIATION SECTION.

			KEYS.
Bars	1——3 (3)	Subject in Alto	D♯ minor
"	3 (3)——6 (1)	Tonal Answer in Treble	A♯ minor
"	6——7	Codetta.	
"	8——10 (3)	Subject in Bass	D♯ minor

MODULATORY SECTION.

"	11——12	Chromatically descending Bass, with florid upper parts.	
"	12 (-1)——14 (4)	Answer in Bass	D♯ minor
"	15——19 (3)	Episode I., modulating from G♯ minor, through D♯ minor, to A♯ minor.	
"	19 (3)——22 (1)	Subject in Alto and in Treble, successively making Stretto I.	A♯ minor
"	23——24	Codetta.	
"	24 (1)——27	Stretto II., Subject in Treble, Alto, and Bass, but slightly altered in all three parts.	
"	27——29 (3)	Stretto III., Subject in Treble, F♯ major. Answer in Alto	F♯ major
"	30——32 (4)	Subject by Inversion in Treble	F♯ major
"	33——36	Episode II., modulating from D♯ minor to G♯ minor.	
"	36——38 (4)	Subject by Inversion in Alto	D♯ minor
"	39——41 (3)	Answer by Inversion in Bass	D♯ minor
"	42——43	Codetta.	
"	43——44 (2)	Subject (altered) in Treble	D♯ minor
"	44 (3)——45 (4)	Subject by Inversion in Bass	D♯ minor
"	45——47 (3)	Stretto IV., Subject by Inversion in Treble	D♯ minor
"	47 (3)——49 (4)	Subject by Inversion in Alto, G♯ minor. Fragment of Subject by inversion in Treble	G♯ minor
"	50——51	Codetta.	
"	52——52	Stretto V. (canonic imitation in the Octave, the parts following one another at the distance of a crotchet).	
"	54——55	Stretto VI. (Subjects inverted).	
"	56——57	Codetta.	
"	57 (-3)——60	Subject in Treble	D♯ minor
"	61 (-3)——64	Subject in Alto	D♯ minor
"	62——67 (1)	Stretto VII., Subject in Bass by Augmentation	D♯ minor
"	64 (3)——67 (½)	Answer by Inversion in Treble	G♯ minor
"	67 (1)——69 (3)	Subject in Bass, F♯ major. Subject in Alto by Augmentation	F♯ major
"	69 (-3)——72 (1)	Subject in Treble	B♯ major
"	72 (4)——75 (2)	Answer in Alto	G♯ minor
"	75 (3)——77	Codetta.	

RECAPITULATORY SECTION.

"	77 (-1)——79 (3)	Stretto VIII., Subject in Bass, D♯ minor. Subject (altered) in Alto ...	D♯ minor
"	77 (3)——82 (4)	Subject by Augmentation in Treble	D♯ minor
"	83——87	Coda, D♯ minor. Final chord major. Tierce de Picardie.	

FUGUE VIII.

SUMMARY.

Exposition: Bars 1 _____ 10.

Counter-exposition: None

Counter-subject: None.

Episodes: Two.

Stretti: Eight (some in Canon).

Inversion: Several instances.

Augmentation: Three instances.

Coda: Bars 83 _____ 87.

REMARKS.

(1.) This Fugue has a " tonal " Answer, and would be styled a " tonal " Fugue. The alteration in the Answer, for the sake of tonality, is made from the second note to the third.

(2.) The Subject appears in its Inverted form for the first time in bar 30 (Treble part).

(3.) The Subject is three times used in Augmentation, (1) in bars 62 in the Bass, (2) in bar 67 in the Alto, (3) in bar 77 in the Treble. The device is thus carried through all three voices.

(4.) In bar 67 the Subjects overlap, the last note of the Subject in Augmentation ends on the first beat of this bar, and becomes the first note of the normal Subject in the same bar.

(5.) Examples of Canonical Imitations will be found in every Stretto. In Stretti I., II., III., IV., VII. and VIII. the Canonical work appears in two of the parts, the third part being either independent or employing some device of the Subject. In Stretto V. the Canonical work appears in all three parts, and in Stretto VI. in all three parts by Inversion.

PRELUDE IX.

SUMMARY.

Bars 1—8, PERIOD I. (ending with a Perfect Cadence in the Dominant).

Bars 9—14, PERIOD II. (ending with a Perfect Cadence in the Tonic, viewed as Dominant of A, in which key the next Period is about to appear).

Bars 15—24, PERIOD III. (reproducing the opening bars in the key of the Subdominant, and gliding back in bar 17 to the Original Tonic).

Bars 23, 24, (Plagal Cadence).

Bars 1, 2 (^{8}), Tonic Pedal.

Bars 15, 16, (^{8}), Subdominant Pedal.

Bars 19, 20, (^{2}), Dominant Pedal.

Bars 22 (^{8}), 23 (^{4}), Tonic Pedal (in the Treble).

REMARKS.

This Prelude is founded upon the following figures :—

In each of the Periods there are momentary subdivisions, in Period I. at bar 4 (^{1}), in II. at bar 13 (^{1}), and in III. at bar 18 (^{1}).

Bar 14 is made to perform a double duty (1) as the concluding bar of Period II., and (2) as a connecting bar to Period III., a Dominant 7th being placed upon it to lead to the key of A major.

PRELUDE IX.
E MAJOR.
SHOWING THE STRUCTURE.

(31)

PRELUDE IX.

Close in Dominant.   PERIOD II.   Modulating   towards   F♯   Minor.

Here it works back to E Major.

PERIOD III. Repetition of Opening Theme in the Subdominant.

Imitation of
fragment of
Opening Theme.   The same.

Gently   returning   to   E.

Imitation of
fragment of
Opening Theme.   The same.

Imitation of frag-
ment of Opening
Theme in Tenor.

FUGUE IX. (E MAJOR).

IN THREE PARTS.

Allegro con brio. ♩ = 108.

ANALYSIS.

ENUNCIATION SECTION.

Bars		Description	KEYS.
1 (-2)	2 (5)	Subject in Alto, ending on first semiquaver of beat 3, bar 2	E
2 (-2)	3 (3)	Real Answer in Treble, entering slightly before the conclusion of Subject, with Counter-subject in Alto	B
3 (-4)	5 (1)	Subject in Bass. Counter-subject in Treble	E
5	6	Codetta.	
6 (-4)	8 (¾)	Subject in Treble. Counter-subject in Bass	E
7 (-4)	9 (¾)	Answer in Alto. Counter-subject in Treble...	B
9 (-4)	10 (4)	Answer in Bass. Counter-subject in Treble	B

MODULATORY SECTION.

Bars		Description	KEYS.
11	12 (2)	Codetta.	
12 (-2)	13 (3)	Subject in Treble	C♯ minor
13 (-3)	16 (-2)	Episode I., modulating from G♯ minor to C♯ minor.	
16 (-2)	17 (3)	Subject in Alto. Counter-subject absent	C♯ minor
17	19	Episode II., modulating from C♯ minor to E.	
19 (-2)	20 (3)	Subject in Bass. Counter-subject absent	E
20 (-2)	21 (2)	Answer in Treble. Counter-subject absent	B
21 (-2)	22 (3)	Subject in Alto. Counter-subject in Treble...	E
22	25	Episode III., modulating from E, sequentially through A and B, back to E.	

RECAPITULATORY SECTION.

Bars		Description	KEYS.
25 (-2)	26 (3)	Subject in Treble. Counter-subject in Alto...	E
26	29	Coda	E
28 (-1)	29	Answer (fragment) in Bass, slightly altered for the conclusion.	

SUMMARY.

Exposition : Bars 1____ 5.
Counter-exposition : Bars 6___ __10.
Episodes : Three.
Stretti : None.
Coda : Bars 26____29.

REMARKS.

(1.) This Fugue has a " real " Answer, and would be called a " real " Fugue

(2.) The Counter-subject is very short, and stands against only a small portion of the Subject, and on three occasions (bars 16, 19, 20) it is altogether omitted.

(3.) The Episodes are constructed from fragments taken sometimes from the Subject and sometimes from the Counter-subject.

(4.) In the Coda a fragment of the Answer is introduced in the Bass to conclude with.

PRELUDE X.

SUMMARY.

Bars **1**—21 (^{1}), PERIOD I. (ending with a Perfect Cadence in the Tonic).

Bars 21—23, EPISODAL (Modulating to the Subdominant, A).

Bars 23—41, PERIOD II. (Presto).

REMARKS.

Period I. has two subdivisions, the first at bar 4, the second at bar 9.

The style of Period I. is that of a solo accompanied by a persistent figure; and it is indeed easy to imagine the solo being played by a Violin or Flute, accompanied either by the under-strings or a Pianoforte:—

Period II., starting with a change of tempo, is in two parts only as far as bar **34, then a third** part is added, and finally it concludes in four-part harmony. The material used in the **construction of this Period is** mainly drawn from the figure used as accompaniment (in the left hand) of the opening **bars of the Prelude.**

In this Prelude fresh artistic devices are built upon one another, showing in fact the **super-position of the** Florid Instrumental Cantilena above the basis of the typical figures and chain of chords as seen in Preludes I. and II., while in its elaborate and impassioned Recitative work it is, in affinity of principle, closely allied to Prelude VIII.

PRELUDE X.

E MINOR.

SHOWING THE STRUCTURE.

PERIOD I. E Minor, establishing the key. From here it works to the Relative Major and settles momentarily

Tonic Pedal.

there. Here it touches upon E Minor, C Major, and gently moves to A Minor. From here

(Sequence of bars 9, 10.)

it gradually returns to E Minor. Two bars modulating to A Minor. PERIOD II.

Here it touches A Minor, C Major, and gradually works home to

E Minor.

Dominant Pedal.

FUGUE X. (E MINOR).

IN TWO PARTS.

ANALYSIS.

ENUNCIATION SECTION.

			KEYS.
Bars 1 — 3 (1)	Subject in Treble, ending on the second quaver of bar 3		E minor
" 3 — 5 (1)	Real Answer in Bass. Counter-subject in Treble		B minor

MODULATORY SECTION.

			KEYS.
" 5 — 11	Episode I., modulating from B minor to G major.		
" 11 — 13 (1)	Subject in Treble. Counter-subject in Bass		G major
" 13 — 15 (⅔)	Answer in Bass. Counter-subject in Treble		D major
" 15 — 20	Episode II., modulating from D major to A minor.		
" 20 — 22 (1)	Subject in Bass. Counter-subject in Treble		A minor
" 22 — 25 (1)	Answer in Treble. Counter-subject in Bass		E minor
" 25 — 30	Episode III., modulating from E minor, through G and A, to D minor.		
" 30 — 32 (1)	Subject in Bass. Counter-subject in Treble		D minor
" 32 — 34 (⅔)	Answer in Treble. Counter-subject in Bass		A minor
" 34 — 38	Episode IV., modulating from A minor to G major in thirty-seventh bar, and a sudden wrench back to E minor in the thirty-eighth bar.		

RECAPITULATORY SECTION.

			KEYS.
" 39 — 40	Fragment of Subject in Treble and of Counter-subject in Bass		E minor
" 40 — 41	Fragment of Subject in Bass		E minor
" 40 — 42	Coda. Imitation of the last part of Subject in Treble		E minor

SUMMARY.

Exposition: Bars 1 — 5.
Counter-exposition: None.
Stretti: None.
Episodes: Four.
Coda: Bars 40 — 42.

REMARKS.

(1.) This Fugue is in two parts. It has a "real" Answer, and would be styled a "real" Fugue.

(2.) Two passages in octaves occur: one at bar 19 — 20 (1), the other at bar 38 — 39 (1). Such passages are not often found in two-part compositions of this class. The first of these marks the point where the balancing second half of the Fugue begins, and the second emphasises the return to the original key at the conclusion.

(3.) All the Episodes are composed of the same materials, and an examination of them will show that Episodes III. and IV. are inversions of Episodes I. and II.

(4.) This Fugue is of very regular construction, being manifestly in two equal halves, the second half, from bar 20, being a transposed inversion of the first half, with short Coda. Moreover, the alternation of passages concerned with Subject matter and Episode is remarkably regular, and the length of each nearly invariable throughout.

PRELUDE XI.

SUMMARY.

Bars 1—8, PERIOD I. (Cadence in the Relative Minor).

Bars 9—15, PERIOD II. (Modulatory)

Bars 15 (^{8})—18, PERIOD III.

REMARKS.

This Prelude is founded upon the following characteristic figure:—

and affords another interesting example of the expansion of the simpler method of Arpeggios (as seen in Preludes I. and II.) into figures more definite and vivid, and demanding a larger amount of space to do their work effectively.

In bar 4 there is a very strong Deceptive Cadence, the ear fully expecting the Tonic chord of F, is deceived by the $\frac{6}{4}$ on its Supertonic, which leads to the key of the Relative Minor.

Bar 10 is in Sequence with bar 9.   In bars 11—12 and 15—16 appear other Sequences with shorter steps.

With only two exceptions, shakes are placed upon all the longer notes (dotted minims) in this Prelude, in order to keep up the volume of tone.

PRELUDE XI.

F MAJOR.

SHOWING THE STRUCTURE.

PERIOD I. F Major, establishing the key. Tonic Pedal.

Forcibly going to the Dominant (C).

Strong Deceptive Cadence to D Min.

Sequence by short

steps.

D Minor.

PERIOD II. Modulatory.

Sequence of bar 9.

Another Sequence, with shorter steps.

Compare Sequence, bars PERIOD III.

11 and 12.

Gently gliding home to F.

8251.

(38)

FUGUE XI. (F MAJOR).

IN THREE PARTS.

Allegretto grazioso. ♩.= 66.

ANALYSIS.

[In analysing this Fugue the first quaver has not been reckoned as a bar.]

ENUNCIATION SECTION.

Bars			KEYS.
Bars 1____4 (¾)	Subject in Alto, ending on the first semiquaver of bar 4		F major
" 4 (8)____8 (¾)	Tonal Answer in Treble. Counter-subject in Alto		C major
" 9 (8)____13 (¾)	Subject in Bass. Counter-subject in Treble		F major
" 13____17	Episode I., modulating from F to C, and back.		
" 17 (8)____21 (¾)	Subject in Treble. Counter-subject divided between the Alto (bar 18) and Bass (19____21)		F major
" 21 (8)____25 (¾)	Answer in Alto. Counter-subject in Treble		C major
" 25 (8)____29 (¾)	Subject in Bass. Counter-subject in Treble		F major
" 27 (8)____31	Stretto I. (incomplete). Subject in Alto. Counter-subject (last part) in Bass		F major

MODULATORY SECTION.

" 31____36	Episode II., modulating from F to D minor.		
" 36 (8)____40 (¾)	Stretto II. (complete). Subject in Treble		D minor
" 38 (8)____42	Subject in Alto		D minor
" 40 (8)____46	Subject in Bass, followed by a Close in D minor		D minor
" 46 (8)____50	Stretto III. (complete). Subject in Bass		G minor
" 48 (8)____52	Subject in Alto		G minor
" 50 (8)____54 (¾)	Subject in Treble		G minor
" 55____56	Close in G minor.		
" 56____63	Episode III., modulating from G minor to F major.		

RECAPITULATORY SECTION.

" 64 (8)____68 (¾)	Stretto IV. (incomplete). Subject in Treble (made more florid)		F major
" 65 (8)____68	Answer in Alto		F major
" 68____72	Coda		F major

SUMMARY.

Exposition : Bars 1____13.
Counter-exposition : Bars 17____31.
Episodes : Three.
Stretti : Four.
Coda : 68____72.

REMARKS.

(1.) This Fugue has a "tonal" Answer, and would be styled a "tonal" Fugue. The alteration in the Answer, for the sake of tonality, is made from the first note to the second.

(2.) The Counter-subject disappears after the Counter-exposition, its place generally being supplied by a florid counterpoint.

(3.) The Episodes are chiefly constructed from the Counter-subject. Episode I. has the Counter-subject in the Bass part (transposed to the dominant C) with syncopations in the two upper parts.

Episode II. has its figures formed from the third bar of the principal subject in the two upper parts, the Bass having a more sustained figure, which commences with a descending sequence.

Episode III. has a new theme in the Alto (bar 56 (-1)) for imitation, mainly taken from the Counter-subject, to which the Treble responds at bar 57 (-1), and this imitative work is continued for two more bars, the Bass meantime gently descending. At bar 60 (-1) the Bass takes up the theme proposed by the Treble in bar 57

PRELUDE XII.

SUMMARY.

Bars 1—12 (³), Period I. (ending with a Perfect Cadence in the Dominant).

Bars 13—22, Period II. (ending in the Tonic, with Major 3rd).

Bars 1, 2 (³), Tonic Pedal.

Bars 17—21, Dominant Pedal.

REMARKS.

This Prelude is built upon the following figures: —

The principal melody is seen in crotchets, and at the opening is supported by notes of similar length in the Tenor. The ornamentation in semiquavers is made up chiefly of Arpeggios, Passing and Auxiliary notes being also employed.

Period I. may be divided into two sections at bar 9 (¹), the Cadence being to the Relative Major (A). Period II. may also be divided at bar 16 (³), at which point there is a Deceptive Cadence, the opening subject being introduced and proceeding upon the Dominant Pedal.

PRELUDE XII.

F MINOR.

SHOWING THE STRUCTURE.

Adagio, con espressione. ♩ = 58.

PERIOD I. F Minor, establishing the key.

From here it moves to the Subdominant Minor (B♭).

Then for contrast to its Relative Major (A♭).

From here

it moves to the Dominant (C). PERIOD II. (Modulatory).

Repetiton of Opening Theme. Dominant Pedal.

Strengthening of the

Dominant, and gradual return home to the Tonic.

FUGUE XII. (F MINOR).

IN FOUR PARTS.

Adagio ma non troppo. ♩ = 69.

sempre legato.

ANALYSIS.

ENUNCIATION SECTION.

			KEYS.
Bars 1 (2) — 4 (¾)	Subject in Tenor		F minor
„ 4 (2) — 7 (¾)	Tonal Answer in Alto, with Counter-subject I. in Tenor		C minor
„ 7 (-1) — 10 (1)	Counter-subject II. in Tenor.		
„ 7 (2) — 10 (1)	Subject in Bass. Counter-subject I. in Alto		F minor
„ 10 (-1) — 13	Codetta formed from Counter-subject I.		
„ 13 (2) — 16	Subject (instead of the usual Answer) in Treble. Counter-subject I. in Bass. Counter-subject II. in Alto...		F minor
„ 16 (-1) — 19	Episode I., modulating from F minor to C minor.		
„ 19 (2) — 22 (1)	Subject in Tenor. Counter-subject I. in Alto, transferred to Treble. Counter-subject II. in Alto (19 (4))		C minor

MODULATORY SECTION.

„ 22 — 27 (3)	Episode II., modulating from C minor to F minor sequentially.		
„ 27 (4) — 30 (3)	Subject in Bass. Counter-subject I. in Tenor. Counter-subject II. in Treble		F minor
„ 30 (-3) — 34 (1)	Episode III., modulating from F minor to A♭ major.		
„ 34 (2) — 37 (1)	Subject in Alto. Counter-subject I. in Treble. Fragment of Counter-subject II. in Tenor		A♭ major
„ 37 — 40 (3)	Episode IV., modulating from F minor to E♭ major.		
„ 40 (4) — 43 (3)	Real Answer in Tenor. Counter-subject I. and Counter-subject II. absent except by short reminiscences		E♭ major
„ 43 (4) — 47 (1)	Episode V., modulating from E♭ major to C minor.		
„ 47 (2) — 50 (½)	Subject in Treble. Counter-subject I. in Alto. Counter-subject II. in Tenor		C minor
„ 50 (-1) — 53 (1)	Episode VI., modulating from C minor to F minor.		

RECAPITULATORY SECTION.

„ 53 (2) — 56 (1)	Subject in Bass. Counter-subject I. in Treble. Counter-subject II. absent		F minor
„ 56 — 58	Coda. Final chord major. Tierce de Picardie.		

SUMMARY.

Exposition : Bars 1 (2) — 16 (1).
Counter-exposition : None.
Stretti : None.
Episodes : Six, all closely allied by use of figures taken from the first Counter-subject and the Codetta.
Coda : Bars 56 — 58.

(42)

FUGUE XII.

REMARKS.

(1.) This Fugue has a "tonal" Answer in the Exposition, and will therefore be called a "tonal" Fugue.

(2.) The order in which the voices enter in the Exposition is unusual, as the Subject and Answer do not regularly alternate, but follow each other in the order: Subject, Answer, Subject, Subject; a Codetta being placed between the last two entries.

(3.) The construction of the Episodes is as follows:—

Episode I. is mainly built upon the first two beats of the Counter-subject I. taken in contrary motion.

Episode II. is built much the same as the first, but the melodic figure used in the Treble of the former is transferred to the Alto.

Episode III. is formed from the Codetta with the addition of a new vivacious figure in the Treble.

Episode IV. is formed in the two upper parts from the Counter-subject I. (the Tenor rests), with a running counterpoint in the Bass part.

Episode V. is on a more extended scale than Episode IV., and all four voices take part in it. The Tenor has a detached figure taken from the second bar of the Counter-subject II.

Episode VI. is built upon the same melodic figures as Episode I., with which it should be compared.

(4.) The Episodes are placed between each *separate* entry of the Subject and Answer, instead of—as is usual—between each *group* of entries.

After the Exposition the Principal Theme appears six times only during forty-two bars, the large space thus allotted to the Episodes proving their great importance in the scheme of this remarkably interesting Fugue.

PRELUDE XIII.

SUMMARY.

Bars 1—12 (¹), PERIOD I. (ending with a Perfect Cadence in the key of the Relative Minor, **D**).

Bars 12—24, PERIOD II. (gently moving to the Minor keys of the Mediant **and** Supertonic, and returning to the original key).

Bars 24—30, PERIOD III. (re-establishing the key).

Bars 26 (³)—28, Dominant Pedal

Bars 24 (³)—30, Coda.

REMARKS.

This Prelude is founded upon the following figures :

In Period I. the Treble leads and the Bass responds, in Period II. the Bass leads and the Treble responds.

At bar 6 (³) the Theme is transposed into the key of the Dominant.

Periods I. and II. are capable of subdivision. In Period I. the division occurs in bar 6, where there is a Perfect Cadence in the Dominant. In Period II. the divisions are (1) in bar 15, where the Cadence is to the Mediant Minor (A♯); (2) at bar 18, where the Cadence is to the Supertonic Minor (G♯); and at bar 24 (³) the Cadence is definitely in the original key, after which the Coda is commenced.

In the early part of the Coda the opening bars are repeated.

PRELUDE XIII
F♯ MAJOR.
SHOWING THE STRUCTURE

PRELUDE XIII.

Opening Theme in the Dominant.

Dominant (C♯).

Free Imit. of Treble.

Here it steadily moves to its

Relative Minor (D♯). PERIOD II. (Modulatory). From here it works on gradually to the Mediant

Minor (A♯), then gently on to its Supertonic Minor (G♯), working

gradually back to the original key, and ending there by a Perfect Cadence in bar 24.

PERIOD III. CODA.

further clenching

Dominant Pedal

the original key.

FUGUE XIII. (F♯ MAJOR).

IN THREE PARTS.

Allegretto. ♩ = 80.

ANALYSIS.

ENUNCIATION SECTION.

				KEYS.
Bars	1 (-1)	3 (¾)	Subject in Treble	F♯
″	3 (-1)	5 (¾)	Tonal Answer in Alto. Counter-subject in Treble	C♯
″	5 (-1)	7 (¾)	Subject in Bass. Counter-subject in Alto	F♯
″	7	11 (3)	Episode I., with a new characteristic figure, modulating from F♯ major to C♯ major.	
″	11 (-3)	13 (3)	Subject in Treble. Counter-subject in Alto...	F♯

MODULATORY SECTION.

″	13	15	Episode II., modulating from F♯ major to C♯ major.	
″	15 (-1)	17	Answer in Alto. Counter-subject in Bass	C♯
″	17	20	Episode III., modulating from C♯ major to D♯ minor.	
″	20 (-1)	22	Subject in Bass. Part of Counter-subject in Alto. Close in D♯ minor...	D♯ minor
″	22	28	Episode IV., modulating from D♯ minor to B major.	
″	28 (-1)	30	Subject in Alto. Counter-subject in Treble replaced by the figure of the Episodes	B major
″	30	31	Treble and Alto contain imitations of the Subject. New figure in the Bass part.	

RECAPITULATORY SECTION.

″	31 (-3)	33 (3)	Subject in Treble. Counter-subject in Bass	F♯ major
″	33 (3)	35	Coda, based on the characteristic figure of the Episodes	F♯ major

SUMMARY.

Exposition : Bars 1____13 (3).
Counter-exposition : None.
Stretti : None.
Episodes : Four.
Coda : Bars 33 (3)____35.

REMARKS.

(1.) This Fugue has a "tonal" Answer, and would be called a "tonal" Fugue. The alteration in the Answer, for the sake of tonality, is made from the first note to the second.

(2.) An entirely new figure appears in the first Episode, which is so frequently employed in various forms from this point to the end that it almost predominates over both Subject and Counter-subject, and towards the end even supplants the Counter-subject as accompaniment to the Subject.

Episode I. A new figure is introduced in the Treble and touched upon by the Alto, but eventually entrusted to the Bass to develop fully, the upper parts moving in sharply contrasted counterpoints.

Episode II. The new figure in the Treble contains in its first few notes a reminiscence of the Subject, imitated by the Alto, the Bass having a florid vivacious figure.

Episode III. Very much the same in construction as Episode I., the florid figure being still entrusted to the Bass.

Episode IV. Long consonant suspensions characterise the Treble and Alto, the florid figure being still assigned to the Bass. At bar 26 this figure is given to the Treble, the Bass and Alto accompanying it in quavers and minims respectively.

PRELUDE XIV.

SUMMARY.

Bars 1—14 (⁸), PERIOD I. (ending in the Dominant Minor, C♯).

Bars 14 (⁴)—24, PERIOD II. (passing through B Minor, then to C♯ Major—its own Dominant, it works home to the original key, bar 22).

Bars 22—24, CODA (using the 1st and 3rd parts of the Th. and again firmly grasping the Tonic key).

REMARKS.

The material used almost exclusively throughout this Prelude is taken from the Theme first given in the **Treble**, which is elaborate, and which for convenience of analysis has been divided into three portions.

Period I. ends at bar 14 (⁸), and not at bar 12 (⁸) as might at first be imagined, the passage between these bars is merely again returning to the same key (C♯ Minor), and only serves to more fully confirm the Cadence already made at bar 12.

Both Periods are capable of subdivision :—Period I. dividing at bar 7 (¹) (Cadence in Relative Major) and Period II. at bar 19 (¹) (Cadence in Dominant Major).

PRELUDE XIV.

F♯ MINOR.

SHOWING THE STRUCTURE.

PRELUDE XIV.

gently working through E Major to its Dominant Minor up to bar 14.

New Episodal figure Modulating to Dominant Minor.

PERIOD II. passes through B Minor,

gradually working on through its Dominant (C♯), and

back again by decided steps to the original

key. CODA.

FUGUE XIV. (F♯ MINOR).

IN FOUR PARTS

Andante con moto. ♩ = 92.

ANALYSIS.

ENUNCIATION SECTION.

			KEYS.
Bars 1 (2) — 4	Subject in Tenor		F♯ minor
" 4 (2) — 7 (1)	Real Answer in Alto, with Counter-subject in Tenor		C♯ minor
" 7 — 8	Codetta.		
" 8 (2) — 11	Subject in Bass. Counter-subject in Alto		F♯ minor
" 11 — 15	Codetta.		
" 15 (2) — 18	Subject in Treble. Counter-subject in Bass...		F♯ minor (irregular

MODULATORY SECTION.

" 18 (2) — 20	Episode I., modulating from F♯ minor to C♯ minor.		
" 20 (5) — 23 (5)	Answer by inversion in Alto. Counter-subject absent		F♯ major
" 23 (6) — 25 (2)	Episode II., modulating from F♯ major to C♯ minor.		
" 25 (3) — 28 (1)	Answer in Treble. Counter-subject in Alto. Close in C♯ minor ...		C♯ minor
" 28 (2) — 29 (1)	Codetta.		
" 29 (2) — 32 (1)	Subject in Tenor. Counter-subject in Treble		F♯ minor
" 32 (2) — 35 (1)	Subject by Inversion in Bass. Counter-subject absent		F♯ minor
" 35 (2) — 37 (1)	Episode III., modulating sequentially from F♯ minor to A major, and back to F♯ minor.		

RECAPITULATORY SECTION.

37 (2) — 40	Subject in Treble. Counter-subject in Alto, with which the Fugue concludes. Tierce de Picardie		F♯ major

SUMMARY.

Exposition : Bars 1 — 18.
Counter-exposition : None.
Episodes : Three.
Stretti : None.

REMARKS.

(1.) This Fugue has a " real " Answer, and would be called a " real " Fugue.

(2.) The order in which the voices enter in the Exposition is unusual, being Subject, Answer, Subject, Subject, instead of the usual Subject, Answer, Subject, Answer. The Exposition is also unusually long, owing to the extent of the Codettas introduced.

(3.) The device of Inversion is used on two occasions, bars 20 and 32. There is no Augmentation or Diminution.

(4.) The figure of the Counter-subject is very characteristic and prominent throughout.

(49)

PRELUDE XV.

SUMMARY.

This Prelude is founded on the following figures:—

Bars 1—11, PERIOD I. (ending with a Perfect Cadence in the key of the Dominant, D).

Bars 11—19, PERIOD II. (gliding to C and D Majors in its early part, and at its conclusion firmly clenching the Tonic key).

Bars 1—3(⁴), Tonic Pedal.

Bars 11—13(³), Dominant Pedal.

REMARKS.

Especially noticeable in the opening bars are the skips of the Octave in the Bass part. These are frequently employed throughout the Prelude, and impart great sprightliness to it.

Period I. may be divided at bar 5, where a new Melody is started in the Treble in the key of the Dominant. Period II. may be more conveniently divided into short Phrases, (1) at bar 12(²), (2) at bar 13(²), (3) at bar 14(²), (4) at bar 15(²), (5) at bar 16(²), the first two Phrases being in a descending Sequence the last three in an ascending Sequence.

PRELUDE XV.

G MAJOR.

SHOWING THE STRUCTURE.

PERIOD I. G Major, establishing the key.

From here it moves away for contrast, touching D major, A minor, and E minor, eventually landing by a Perfect Cadence on the Dominant (D). PERIOD II. Persistency of the Dominant Pedal. Here it touches G Major, C Major, then D Major, then working homewards, it firmly stamps in the mind the Tonic key.

Dominant Pedal.

FUGUE XV. (G MAJOR).

IN THREE PARTS.

ANALYSIS.

ENUNCIATION SECTION.

			KEYS.
Bars	1 _____ 5 (1)	Subject in Treble	G
"	5 _____ 9 (1)	Real Answer in Alto	D
"	5 (2) __ 6 (4)	Codetta in Treble.	
"	6 (5) __ 8 (4)	Counter-subject in Treble.	
"	9 (2) __ 11	Codetta.	
"	11 _____ 15 (1)	Subject in Bass. Counter-subject in Alto	G
"	15 (2) __ 20 (1)	Episode I., modulating from G to C, and back to G.	
"	20 (2) __ 24	Subject by Inversion in Alto. Counter-subject (incomplete) by Inversion in Bass	G
"	24 _____ 28	Answer by Inversion in Treble. Counter-subject by Inversion in Alto ...	D
"	28 _____ 31	Subject by Inversion in Bass. Counter-subject (incomplete) by Inversion in Treble	G

MODULATORY SECTION.

"	31 _____ 38	Episode II., modulating from G to E minor.	
"	38 _____ 42 (1)	Subject in Treble	E minor
"	40 _____ 42	Counter-subject in Alto.	
"	42 _____ 43	Codetta.	
"	43 _____ 46	Subject by Inversion in Alto. Counter-subject by Inversion in Treble ...	E minor
"	46 _____ 51	Episode III., modulating from E minor to B minor.	
"	51 _____ 54	Subject in Treble	B minor
"	52 _____ 54	Stretto I. (incomplete). Subject in Bass	B minor
"	54 _____ 60	Episode IV., modulating from B minor to D major.	
"	60 (4) __ 62	Subject in Alto. Counter-subject absent	D major
"	61 (4) __ 64 (1)	Stretto II. (incomplete). Subject in Treble, on pedal A	D major
"	64 _____ 69	Episode V.	
"	69 (4) __ 73 (1)	Subject by Inversion in Bass. Counter-subject in Alto	G major
"	73 (2) __ 77	Episode VI.	
"	77 _____ 79	Subject by Inversion in Alto	G
"	78 _____ 79	Stretto III. (complete). Subject by Inversion in Bass	G

RECAPITULATORY SECTION.

"	79 _____ 82	Subject in Treble, accompanied in 3rds below by the first part of Subject in Alto	G
"	82 _____ 86	Coda, the last two bars of which are on Tonic pedal	G

SUMMARY.

Exposition : Bars 1 _____ 15 (1).
Counter-exposition : Bars 20 _____ 81 (1).
Episodes : Six.
Stretti : Three.
Inversion : Several instances.
Coda : 82 _____ 86.

FUGUE XV.

REMARKS.

(1.) This Fugue has a "real" Answer, and would be called a "real" Fugue.

(2.) The Counter-subject appears somewhat late—not until the second half of the second bar of the Answer.

(3.) Free inversion is applied to the Subject and Counter-subject.

(4.) All the Episodes are formed from the new figure used in the Codetta (bars 5———6), sometimes with the addition of a free part.

Episode I. is in a descending sequence with an additional new counterpoint in the Treble.

Episode II. is also in a descending sequence. The figure employed in the Treble of Episode I. is here given to the Bass, and the Bass of Episode I. to the Treble. Ornamental scale passages are introduced in the Treble at bars 34 and 37 and in the Bass at bars 35 and 36, the Alto having a detached figure.

Episode III. contains notes of greater length in the Treble, and florid work in the two under parts.

Episode IV. The first bar of the Codetta figure is inverted and used in 3rds with the Bass. Demi-semiquavers are also introduced. In bar 56 the Alto enters in imitation at the 4th below.

Episode V. Here the Bass has a detached figure, the upper parts being much the same as in Episode II.

Episode VI. is in two parts only, the vigorous scale passages being again introduced.

PRELUDE XVI.

SUMMARY.

This Prelude is founded upon the following figures:—

Bars 1—7, PERIOD I. (ending with a Perfect Cadence in the relative Major).

Bars 7—11, PERIOD II. (ending with a Perfect Cadence in the Subdominant).

Bars 11—19, PERIOD III. (passing back to the Original key, which it grasps firmly with the Tonic Pedal in the last two bars).

Bars 14—15 (^{3}), Dominant Pedal.

Bars 18,—19, Tonic Pedal, forming Coda.

REMARKS.

Four contrasted figures are used in the compositions of this Prelude:—

(1) A sustained note with the shake.

(2) A short arpeggio figure (see bar 1. Tenor part).

(3) An ornamental figure including two demi-semiquavers (see bar 2).

(4) A figure mostly appearing in four demi-semiquavers (see bars 8 and 9 in the two upper parts).

Figure 3, quoted above is also employed by Free Inversion, compare bar 6 (Treble part) and bar 8 (Bass part) with bar 2.

In Period I. there is a momentary division at bar 6 (^{1}) (F Major).

In Period III. there is a division at bar 18 where the Coda is reached.

PRELUDE XVI.

G MINOR.

SHOWING THE STRUCTURE.

Adagio ma non troppo. ♪ = 120.

PERIOD I. G Minor, confirming the key.

From here it further stresses the Tonic key. Passing through F Major to its own Relative Major (B♭). PERIOD II.

Sequence (descending). Moving to C Minor. PERIOD III.

Gently

returning home to the Tonic. CODA.

Dominant Pedal.

Tonic Pedal.

FUGUE XVI. (G MINOR).

IN FOUR PARTS.

Andante con moto. ♩ = 84.

ANALYSIS.

ENUNCIATION SECTION.

				KEYS.
Bars	1 .(-1)___2 (3)	Subject in Alto		G minor
"	2 (-3)___4 (½)	Tonal Answer in Treble, with Counter-subject in Alto		D minor
"	4_____5	Codetta.		
"	5 (-1)___6 (3)	Subject in Bass. Counter-subject in Treble		G minor
"	6 (-3)___8 (½)	Answer in Tenor. Counter-subject in Bass...		D minor

MODULATORY SECTION.

"	8_____12	Episode I., modulating from D minor to Close in G minor, and then to B♭ major and Close.		
"	12 (-1)___13 (3)	Subject in Alto. Counter-subject in Tenor		B♭ major
"	13 (-3)___15	Answer in Bass. Counter-subject in Tenor...		F major
"	15 (-1)___16	Answer in Treble. Counter-subject in Bass		F major
"	17 (-1)___18 (3)	Subject in Bass. Counter-subject in Treble		B♭ major
"	17 (-3)___19	Stretto I. Answer in Alto		E♭ major
"	20 (-1)___21 (3)	Subject in Bass. Counter-subject in Alto		C minor
"	21 (-3)___23	Subject in Treble. Counter-subject (slightly altered) in Bass		C minor
"	23 (-1)___24 (3)	Answer in Alto. Counter-subject in Treble, with Close in G minor ...		G minor
"	24 (3)___28	Episode II., modulating from G minor through E♭ major, and back to G minor.		

RECAPITULATORY SECTION.

"	28 (-1)___29	Stretto II. Subject in Treble. Counter-subject in Alto. Subject in Tenor		G minor
"	29 (-1)___30	Subject in Bass		G minor
"	31 (-3)___33 (1)	Subject in Alto		G minor
"	32 (-1)___33	Counter-subject in Bass.		
"	33_____34	Subject in Tenor, with which the Fugue ends, without Coda. Tierce de Picardie		G major

SUMMARY.

Exposition : Bars 1_____8.
Counter-exposition : None.
Episodes : Two.
Stretti : Two.
Pedal : None.

REMARKS.

(1.) This Fugue has a " Tonal " Answer, and would be called a " Tonal " Fugue. The alteration in the Answer, for the sake of tonality, is made from the first note to the second.

(2.) Episode I. is built upon the second limb of the Subject. Episode II. has a new figure, alternating in the Treble and Alto, but the Bass is built upon the same portion of the Subject as Episode I.

(3.) Both Strettos are incomplete—i.e., all the voices do not take part in them.

PRELUDE XVII.

SUMMARY.

Bars 1—18, PERIOD I. (ending with a Perfect Cadence in the key of the Dominant E♭).

Bars 18—44, PERIOD II. (beginning on the Dominant, and ending with a Perfect Cadence in the key of the Tonic, A♭).

Bars 35—44, CODA (further confirmation of the Original key.)

REMARKS.

This Prelude is constructed chiefly upon the figure used in the Treble of bar 1.

Period I. has a subdivision at bar 9.

At the beginning of Period II. the Theme is started in the key of the Dominant.

The Coda is constructed upon Free Imitations of the Theme in a descending Sequence

PRELUDE XVII.

A♭ MAJOR.

SHOWING THE STRUCTURE.

PRELUDE XVII.

(Musical score)

moves   gradually   to   the   contrasting   key,   the   Dominant,   and   ends   there   by   a

Sequence (ascending).

perfect   Cadence.   *Th. in Bass, in the Dominant.*
PERIOD II.

Free Imit. of Th.

Imit. of Th. (descending Sequence).

Here   it   moves   back   to   A♭.   Then   to   D♭,   gradually   working

Th.

back to A♮ (bar 35).

CODA.   *Th. in Sequence (descending).*

FUGUE XVII. (A♭ MAJOR).

IN FOUR PARTS.

Andante con espress. ♩ = 63.

legato.

ANALYSIS.

ENUNCIATION SECTION.

Bars				KEYS
Bars	1$^{(2)}$—2$^{(1)}$	Subject in Tenor...		A♭
"	2$^{(2)}$—3$^{(¾)}$	Tonal Answer in Bass, with free Counter-subject in Tenor		E♭
"	3$^{(2)}$—5	Codetta.		
"	5$^{(2)}$—6	Subject in Treble. Part of Counter-subject in Bass		A♭
"	6$^{(2)}$—7$^{(1)}$	Answer in Alto. Counter-subject absent		E♭
"	7$^{(2)}$—10$^{(1)}$	Episode I., modulating from E♭ to A♭.		
"	10$^{(2)}$—11$^{(1)}$	Subject in Tenor. Counter-subject (varied) in Bass		A♭

MODULATORY SECTION.

"	11$^{(2)}$—13	Episode II., modulating from A♭ to F minor.		
"	13$^{(2)}$—14	Subject in Alto. Counter-subject (varied) in Tenor		F minor
"	14—17	Episode III., modulating, after close in F minor, to B♭ minor.		
"	17$^{(2)}$—18	Subject in Tenor. Counter-subject absent		B♭ minor
"	18$^{(2)}$—19	Answer in Alto		B♭ minor
"	19—21	Episode IV., modulating from B♭ minor to A♭ major.		
"	21—22	Fragment of Subject in Alto and of Answer in Treble.		
"	23$^{(2)}$—24$^{(1)}$	Answer in Alto (altered at 5th note). Counter-subject in Tenor...		A♭
"	24$^{(2)}$—25$^{(1)}$	Subject in Treble. Counter-subject in Tenor		E♭
"	24$^{(4)}$—25	Subject (varied) in Alto and developed into a sequence of suspended 9ths		A♭
"	25$^{(2)}$—27	Episode V., modulating sequentially from D♭ to A♭.		
"	27$^{(2)}$—28$^{(1)}$	Subject in Bass		A♭
"	28$^{(2)}$—29	Answer in Tenor...		C minor
"	29$^{(2)}$—30	Answer in Alto. Free version of Counter-subject in Tenor		A♭
"	30$^{(2)}$—31	Answer in Treble		D♭

RECAPITULATORY SECTION.

"	31—35	Coda		A♭
"	33$^{(4)}$—34$^{(3)}$	Subject in Treble		A♭
"	35	Counter-subject (reminiscence of) in Alto		A♭

SUMMARY.

Exposition: Bars 1——7.	Stretti: None.
Counter-exposition: None.	Pedal: None.
Episodes: Five.	Coda: Bars 31, 35.

REMARKS.

(1.) This Fugue has a "tonal" Answer, and would be called a "tonal" Fugue. The alteration in the Answer, for the sake of tonality, is made from the second note to the third.

(2.) The free Counter-subject is occasionally dispensed with and a new melody substituted for it, thus imparting additional interest and variety to the Fugue.

(3.) The following is a description of the Episodes, which for the most part are founded upon the free Counter-subject, but other figures of melody are occasionally added:—

Episode I. Built upon the Counter-subject in the Alto and imitated by the Bass in the 8ve, a contrasted counterpoint being given to the Treble.

Episode II. Free imitation of the Subject in the Bass. Suspensions in the Tenor, with ornamental counterpoint in the Treble.

Episodes III, IV. These retain the melodic figures of Episode II, but transferred to different voices (observe, Episode III. is distant one bar only from Episode II.).

Episode V. Suspended figures in the two upper parts with a running Tenor founded on the Counter-subject.

(4.) The entries in bars 21, 27——30 do not constitute real Stretti, because they do not overlap each other.

PRELUDE XVIII.

SUMMARY.

This Prelude is founded upon the following figure :—

Bars 1—13 (¹), PERIOD I. (ending with a Perfect Cadence in the Dominant Minor, D♯).

Bars 13—29, PERIOD II. (starting from D♯ Minor, with the Theme in the Bass part).

Bars 27—29, CODA (using for foundation the Theme in the Bass part, in Tonic key).

Bars 28, 29, PLAGAL CADENCE. Final Chord, Tierce de Picardié.

REMARKS.

The figure mostly employed for the material of this Prelude is seen in the Treble bars 1, 2 (¹). It is used at the following important points as well as at other places, (1) at bar 6 in the Relative Major (Bass part); (2) at bar 13 in the Dominant Minor (Bass part); (3) at bar 18 in the Subdominant Minor (Treble part); (4) at bar 27 (Bass part), imitated in Contrary Motion by the Alto in bar 28.

In both Periods there are subdivisions. In Period I. at bar 5 (¹) (Cadence in Relative Major), and in Period II. at bar 18 (¹) (Cadence in the Subdominant Minor).

PRELUDE XVIII.
G♯ MINOR.
SHOWING THE STRUCTURE.

PRELUDE XVIII

Here it moves through F♯ Minor to C♯ Minor, and returns to the Tonic Minor. From here it stretches on to the Dominant Minor, and confirms this key. From here it returns to G♯ Minor, again touching C♯ Minor, and by a series of suspensions works gently homewards to G♯ Minor. Here it further confirms the Tonic, and ends in it by a Perfect Cadence. Coda.

Period II.

FUGUE XVIII. (G♯ MINOR).

IN FOUR PARTS.

Andante con espressione. ♩ = 60.

ANALYSIS.

ENUNCIATION SECTION.

Bars		Description	KEYS.
1 (2)	3 (⅔)	Subject in Tenor	G♯ minor
" 3 (2)	5 (⅔)	Tonal Answer in Alto, with Counter-subject in Tenor	D♯ minor
" 5 (2)	7 (⅔)	Subject in Treble. Counter-subject in Alto	G♯ minor
" 7 (2)	9	Answer in Bass. Counter-subject in Treble	D♯ minor
" 9	11	Episode I., modulating from G♯ minor to D♯ minor and Close.	
" 11 (2)	13	Answer in Tenor. Counter-subject in Treble	D♯ minor
" 13	15	Episode II., modulating from G♯ minor to C♯ minor and Close.	
" 15 (2)	17	Real Answer in Bass. Counter-subject in Alto	C♯ minor
" 17 (2)	19	Subject in Tenor. Counter-subject absent	G♯ minor
" 19 (2)	21	Answer in Alto. Counter-subject in Tenor	D♯ minor

MODULATORY SECTION.

" 21	24	Episode III., modulating from G♯ minor to D♯ minor.	
" 24 (2)	26	Subject in Treble. Counter-subject absent	D♯ minor
" 26 (2)	28	Answer in Bass. Counter-subject absent	F♯ minor
" 28	32	Episode IV., modulating from B to G♯ minor and Close.	

RECAPITULATORY SECTION.

" 32 (2)	34	Subject in Tenor. Counter-subject in Alto	G♯ minor
" 34	37	Episode V., modulating from D♯ minor to C♯ minor.	
" 37 (2)	39	Answer in Treble. Counter-subject (reminiscence of) in Alto	D♯ minor
" 39	41	Coda	G♯ minor

SUMMARY.

Exposition : Bars 1 (2) __ 9 (1)   Stretti : None.
Counter-exposition : Bars 11 __ 17.   Pedal : None.
Episodes : Five.   Coda : Bars 39 __ 41.

REMARKS.

(1.) This Fugue has a "tonal" Answer, and would be called a "tonal" Fugue. The alteration in the Answer, for the sake of tonality, is made from the first note to the second.

(2.) In bar 15 the Answer is exceptional, being Real instead of Tonal.

(3.) The Counter-subject is absent on three occasions (see Analysis).

(4.) The following is a brief description of the Episodes :—

Episode I. is formed in the Bass from the second limb of the Subject in an ascending sequence. Plain harmonies only are used in the three upper parts.

Episode II. is formed in the Treble from the first limb of the Subject taken in contrary motion, the second limb being given to the Tenor, and suspensions to the Alto.

Episode III. is built mainly upon a new characteristic figure proposed by the Bass and imitated in the fifth above by the Alto, the Tenor part being independent. The Treble rests.

Episode IV. is built upon precisely the same figure as Episode III., but placed in different voices— here Alto and Treble—the Bass part being independent. The Tenor rests.

Episode V. is formed mainly from the second limb of the Subject.

PRELUDE XIX.

SUMMARY.

Bars 1—14 (^{8}), Period I. (ending with a Perfect Cadence in the key of the Relative Minor, F$\sharp$).

Bars 14 (^{4})—24, Period II. (Modulatory in early part).

REMARKS.

Three Themes are used in the construction of this Prelude. Theme I. starts at once in bar 1 in the Treble part, Theme II. at bar 1 (^{2}) in the Bass part, and Theme III. at bar 1 (—^{4}) in the Middle part.

At bars 4 (^{1}) and 17 (^{8}) Themes II. and III. are used above Theme I. Two other varieties are notice·able, (1) at bar 8 (^{8}), where Theme I. is placed in the Middle part, Theme II. being above and Theme III. below it ; (2) at bar 20, where Theme I. is at the top, Theme II. in the Middle and Theme III. at the bottom. These Themes are therefore constructed with each other according to the rules of Triple Counterpoint.

In the early part of Period II. the material employed is taken from Theme III. chiefly, scale passages being placed below it, leading to the repetition of all three Themes in the original key at bar 17.

PRELUDE XIX.

A MAJOR.

SHOWING THE STRUCTURE

(in a descending Sequence) to Th. in
Tonic at bar 8 (³).

Th. I. in Tonic.

Th. III.

Th. in the Relative Minor.

Episode leading to Relative Minor.

Th. III.

Th. II.

PERIOD II., passing through B Major, E Major, and back to

the Tonic.

Th. III.

Th. II.

Th. I.

Th. I.

Th. II.

Th. III.

(64)

FUGUE XIX. (A MAJOR).

IN THREE PARTS.

Allegretto. $\quad \downarrow . = 69.$

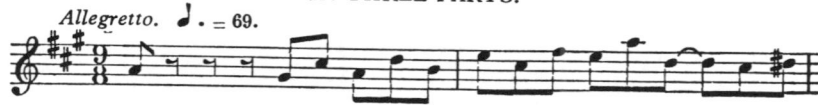

ANALYSIS.

ENUNCIATION SECTION.

Bars				KEYS.
1 —— 2 (5)	Subject in Treble	... ...		A
" 2 —— 3 (5)	Tonal Answer in Alto	... ...		E
" 4 —— 5 (5)	Subject in Bass	... ...		A
" 6 —— 7 (5)	Answer in Bass	... ...		E
" 8 —— 9	Codetta, and Close in A.			
" 9 —— 10 (5)	Subject in Treble	... ...		A

MODULATORY SECTION.

" 11 —— 12	Episode I., modulating from A to F♯ minor and Close.			
" 13 —— 14 (5)	Subject in Bass			F♯ minor
" 16 —— 17 (8)	Subject in Bass			E
" 17 —— 23	Episode II., modulating from A to E, and closing in that key, and then back to A.			
" 23 —— 24 (5)	Subject in Bass, with new and more rapid passage in Alto			A
" 25 —— 26 (5)	Answer in Alto			A
" 27 —— 28 (5)	Answer in Alto			E
" 29 —— 31	Episode III., modulating from E, through A, to D.			
" 31 —— 32 (5)	Subject in Alto, and Close in D			D
" 33 —— 34 (5)	Subject in Bass, chromatically altered			B minor
" 34 —— 39	Episode IV., modulating from B minor to F♯ minor.			
" 39 (5) —— 40	Answer (altered) in Bass, and close in F♯ minor			F♯ minor
" 42 —— 43 (5)	Subject in Alto			A
" 44 —— 45 (5)	Answer (altered) in Bass			E
" 46 —— 54	Coda, comprising frequent imitations of the Subject.			

SUMMARY.

Exposition: Bars 1——7.
Counter-exposition: None.
Episodes: Four.
Stretti: None.
Pedal: None.
Coda: Bars 46——54.

REMARKS.

(1.) This Fugue has a "tonal" Answer, and would be called a "tonal" Fugue. The alteration in the Answer, for the sake of tonality, is made from the first note to the second.

(2.) The Answer in the Alto (bar 2) enters before the conclusion of the Subject in the Treble, which in the Exposition is unusual.

(3.) An Answer appears in the Bass (bar 6) almost immediately after the Subject in the same voice. The same occurs in the Alto (bars 25——27).

(4.) The Subject is only found twice in the Treble (bars 1 and 9), after that it entirely disappears from this part.

(5.) It has no Counter-subject.

(6.) The Episodes are constructed from material taken from the Subject.

This Fugue is somewhat free in construction. There is no *Thematic* Recapitulation proper.

PRELUDE XX.

SUMMARY.

Bars 1—13, PERIOD I. (Ending with a Perfect Cadence in the Relative Major, C).

Bars 13—22, PERIOD II. (Modulatory to bar 20, then gently curving round to the Tonic).

Bars 22—28, PERIOD III. (starting with the Theme (varied) in the Tonic key).

Bars 26—28, TONIC PEDAL AND CODA (firmly grasping the Tonic key).

REMARKS.

This Prelude is constructed upon the Theme used in the Treble, the three component figures of which appear in bar 1.

The Periods are capable of subdivisions. Period I. may be divided into three sections at bars 4 and 8. Period II. into two sections at bar 20, and Period III. into two sections at bar 26, where the Coda begins.

PRELUDE XX.

A MINOR.

SHOWING THE STRUCTURE.

(66)

PRELUDE XX.

times in a descending Sequence.

Th. in the Relative Major (commencing on the 3rd of the Tonic).

PERIOD II.

From here it moves away, touching upon G Minor, then

upon D Minor, and gently works homewards to the Tonic.

Th. in the Subdominant. Same varied.

Th. in Tonic. Same varied.

PERIOD III.

CODA.

Tonic Pedal.

FUGUE XX. (A minor).

IN FOUR PARTS.

Andante con moto. ♩ = 72.

ANALYSIS.

ENUNCIATION SECTION.

					KEYS.
Bars	1 (-1) — 4 (1)	Subject in Alto			A minor
"	4 (-1) — 7 (¾)	Real Answer in Treble			E minor
"	7 — 8	Codetta.			
"	8 (-1) — 11 (¾)	Subject in Bass			A minor
"	11 (-1) — 14 (1)	Answer in Tenor			E minor

MODULATORY SECTION.

					KEYS.
"	14 (-3) — 17 (1)	Subject by Inversion in Treble			G major
"	17 (-3) — 18 (3)	Subject (first part) by Inversion in Alto			G major
"	18 (-1) — 20 (3)	Subject by Inversion in Tenor...			G major
"	21 (-1) — 23 (3)	Subject by Inversion in Bass			D minor
"	24 (-1) — 26 (3)	Subject by Inversion in Alto			A minor
"	27 (-3) — 30 (3)	Subject in Treble } in Stretto			A minor
"	28 (-1) — 31	Subject in Tenor }			A minor
"	31 (-3) — 34 (3)	Answer in Alto } in Stretto			E minor
"	32 (-1) — 35 (¾)	Answer in Bass }			E minor
"	36 (-3) — 39 (3)	Subject in Tenor } in Stretto			A minor
"	37 (-1) — 40 (1)	Subject in Alto }			A minor
"	39 (3) — 43	Episode I. (unusually late for its *first* appearance), modulating from A minor to C major.			
"	43 (-1) — 46 (1)	Subject in Treble } in Stretto			C
"	43 (-3) — 46 (3)	Subject in Bass }			C
"	45 (-4) — 47 (1)	Subject (second part) in Tenor			C
"	46 (-4) — 48	Subject (second part) in Alto			C
"	48 (-3) — 51 (2)	Answer by Inversion in Alto } in Stretto			D minor
"	49 (-1) — 52	Answer by Inversion in Tenor, and Codetta }			D minor
"	53 (-1) — 56 (1)	Subject in Bass } in Stretto			G major
"	53 (-3) — 56 (3)	Subject in Treble and Codetta }			G major
"	57 (-3) — 60	Subject by Inversion in Treble } in Stretto			A minor
"	58 (-1) — 62	Subject by Inversion in Alto, and Codetta }			A minor
"	62 (-1) — 63 (3)	Answer by Inversion in Bass } in Stretto			A minor
"	62 (-3) — 63 (3)	Answer by Inversion in Tenor }			A minor
"	64 (-3) — 67 (3)	Subject in Bass } in Stretto			D minor
"	65 (-1) — 68 (1)	Answer in Tenor }			A minor
"	67 (-3) — 70 (3)	Answer by Inversion in Treble } in Stretto			A minor
"	68 (-1) — 70 (4)	Subject by Inversion in Alto }			D minor
"	71 — 73	Episode II., modulating from D minor to F major.			
"	73 (-1) — 75 (3)	Subject by Inversion in Bass } in Stretto			F major
"	73 (-3) — 76	Subject by Inversion in Alto }			F major
"	76 (-1) — 77 (3)	Answer by Inversion in Tenor } in Stretto			C major
"	77 (-1) — 78 (3)	Subject in Alto }			D minor
"	77 (-3) — 78 (3)	Subject in Treble }			D minor
"	79	Codetta and Pause.			
"	80 (-3) — 82 (1)	Subject in Alto } in Stretto			A minor
"	81 (-1) — 82 (3)	Answer in Treble }			E
"	83 (-3) — 86	Tonic Pedal. Three upper parts in Stretto...			A
"	86 — 87	Coda and continuation of Tonic Pedal. Close on Tonic Major			A major

FUGUE XX.

SUMMARY.

Exposition: Bars 1——14.

Counter-exposition: None.

Counter-subject: None.

Episodes: Two.

Owing to the structure of the Subject, special interest is given to the Fugue by the manner in which the quotations of it constantly overlap in a kind of Canonic Stretto. (See Analysis.)

Inversion: Many instances.

Pedals: Three. (1.) Dominant, 60——62. (2.) On the Dominant of the relative major, 76——77 (3.) On the Tonic, 83——87.

REMARKS.

(1.) This Fugue has a "real" Answer, and would be styled a "real" Fugue.

(2.) The devices of Inversion and Canonical Imitation abound in this Fugue to such an extent as to give it a special character.

(3.) Episode I. is constructed upon the Subject, but Episode II. of new material.

(4.) This Fugue has three short Pedal points. The first on the Dominant (E), the second on the Dominant of the Relative Major (G), and the third on the Tonic (A).

The latter part of this Fugue is somewhat irregular in form, fragments of the Subject being introduced in the Subdominant minor, D. (83——86), in order to suggest the major conclusion which is about to follow.

PRELUDE XXI.

SUMMARY.

This Prelude is constructed upon the following figures: —

Bars 1—10, PERIOD I. (ending with a Perfect Cadence in the key of the Dominant, F.).

Bars 10—20, PERIOD II. (Modulatory).

Bars 18—20, CODA (confirming the Tonic key).

REMARKS.

Period I. cannot be subdivided. In Period II. there is a division at bar 18, where the Coda is commenced.

The difference in character and style of the two Periods is mainly due to the employment of a new contrasting figure which first appears in bar 11 (^{2}).

This Prelude divides exactly into two halves.

PRELUDE XXI.

(B♭ MAJOR.)

SHOWING THE STRUCTURE.

Allegro vivace. ♩ = 80.

PERIOD I. B♭ Major, establishing the key.

Ascending Sequence (3—5 (³).

From here it moves away   to   F Major

Ascending Sequence (6—8 (¹).

for contrast.

And   ultimately

lands   in   F   Major.   PERIOD II. (Modulatory).

Returning   to

B♭ Major.   CODA.

FUGUE XXI. (B♭ MAJOR).

IN THREE PARTS.

Allegretto scherzoso. ♩ = 116.

ANALYSIS.

ENUNCIATION SECTION.

			KEYS.
Bars	1 (-1) — 5 (¾)	Subject in Treble	B♭
"	5 (-1) — 9 (¾)	Tonal Answer in Alto, with Counter-subject in Treble	F
"	9 (-1) — 13 (¾)	Subject in Bass. Counter-subject I. in Alto	B♭
"	9 (3) — 13 (¾)	Counter-subject II. in Treble.	
"	13 (-1) — 17 (¾)	Answer in Treble. Counter-subject I. in Bass. Counter-subject II. in Alto	F

MODULATORY SECTION.

"	17 — 22	Episode I., modulating from F to G minor.	
"	22 (-1) — 26 (¾)	Subject in Alto. Counter-subject I. in Treble. Counter-subject II. in Bass	G minor
"	26 (-1) — 30 (¾)	Answer in Bass. Counter-subject I. in Alto. Counter-subject II. in Treble	C minor
"	30 — 35	Episode II., from C minor, through G, and back to C minor.	
"	35 (-1) — 37 (¾)	Answer in Alto. Counter-subject I. in Treble. Counter-subject II. in Bass	E♭ major
"	37 (-1) — 41 (¾)	Subject in Treble. Counter-subject I. in Alto. Counter-subject II. in Bass	E♭ major

RECAPITULATORY SECTION.

"	41 (-1) — 45 (¾)	Answer in Alto. Counter-subject I. in Treble. Counter-subject II. in Bass	B♭ major
"	45 (1) — 48	Coda	B♭ major

SUMMARY.

Exposition : Bars 1 —— 13.
Counter-exposition : None.
Episodes : Two.
Stretti : None.
Coda : Bars 45 —— 48.

REMARKS.

(1.) This Fugue has a "tonal" Answer, and would be called a "tonal" Fugue. The alteration in the Answer, for the sake of tonality, is made from the first note to the second.

(2.) Triple counterpoint is employed, because there are two Counter-subjects to be worked above and below the Subject and Answer.

(3.) Counter-subject II. appears in the Bass part three times in succession (bars 35 —— 44).

(4.) The two Episodes, though short, are exceedingly interesting.

Episode I. is written in a descending sequence, and is formed in the Bass on bar 3 (4) of the Subject, continuing as far as bar 19, the Treble and Alto having a florid counterpoint founded also on the latter part of the Subject. At bar 19 (-1 — 22 (¾) the Bass is an inversion of the first six notes of the Subject, the Treble continuing the florid counterpoint and the Alto being silent.

Episode II is an inversion of Episode I. with the addition of an independent part in the Alto.

8251.   (72)

PRELUDE XXII.

SUMMARY.

Bars 1—13, PERIOD I. (ending with a Perfect Cadence in the key of the Dominant Minor, F).
Bars 13—24, PERIOD II. (Modulatory in its early part).

Bars 1—3, Tonic Pedal.
Bars 20—22, Dominant Pedal.
Bars 23(^{3}), 24, Tonic Pedal.

REMARKS.

This Prelude is mainly built upon the Opening figure (Treble part), which is frequently used in Contrary Motion, especially in PERIOD II.

At bar 7(^{3}) the Theme appears in the Treble in a descending Sequence, and at bar 13 a new figure appears in the Bass, also working in a descending Sequence. In the same Sequence also the Opening figure is used for the upper parts.

PRELUDE XXII.

B♭ MINOR.

This Prelude is copied out somewhat fully in order to show the Melodic features as pointedly as possible.

PRELUDE XXII.

From here it gradually works away, and makes for its Dominant Minor, and ultimately lands there by a Perfect Cadence. Period II. Here it touches E♭ Minor, A♭ Major, D♭ Major, working gradually back to the original key.

Dominant Pedal.

Return to the Tonic.

Tonic Pedal.

FUGUE XXII. (B♭ MINOR).

IN FIVE PARTS.

Adagio ma non troppo. ♩ 120.

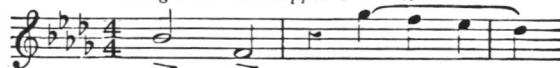

ANALYSIS.

ENUNCIATION SECTION.

			KEYS.
Bars	1——3 (1)	Subject in First Treble	B♭ minor
"	3——5 (1)	Tonal Answer in Second Treble	F minor
"	5 (2)—10	Codetta.	
"	10——12 (1)	Subject in Alto	B♭ minor
"	12——14 (1)	Answer in Tenor	F minor
"	15——17 (1)	Subject in Bass	B♭ minor

MODULATORY SECTION.

"	17 (2)—25	Episode I., modulating from B♭ minor to D♭ major.	
"	25——27 (1)	Subject in First Treble	D♭
"	27——29 (1)	Answer in Second Treble	E♭ minor
"	29——31 (1)	Subject in Tenor	B♭ minor
"	32——34 (1)	Answer in Bass	E♭ minor
"	34——36	Codetta.	
"	37——39 (1)	Answer in Alto	D♭ major
"	39 (2)—46	Episode II., modulating sequentially from A♭, through E♭, to B♭ minor.	
"	46 (2)—48 (½)	Answer in Tenor	B♭ minor
"	48——50 (1)	Answer in Bass	B♭ minor
"	50——52 (2)	Answer in First Treble ...	E♭ minor
"	50 (3)—52 (3)	Answer in Second Treble	E♭ minor
"	51——53 (2)	Subject in Alto } Stretto I. (complete)	E♭ minor
"	52——54	Answer (slightly altered) in Bass	E♭ minor
"	53——55 (1)	Answer in Tenor	E♭ minor
"	55——57 (1)	Subject in Second Treble. Answer in Alto	E♭ minor
"	57 (2)—67	Episode III., modulating from E♭ minor to B♭ minor.	

RECAPITULATORY SECTION.

"	67 (3)—69 (3)	Subject in First Treble	B♭ minor
"	68——70 (1)	Answer in Second Treble	B♭ minor
"	68 (3)—70 (3)	Subject in Alto } Stretto II. (complete)	B♭ minor
"	69——71 (1)	Answer in Tenor	B♭ minor
"	69 (3)—71 (3)	Subject in Bass	B♭ minor
"	72——75	Coda.	
"	73 (1)—74	Reminiscence of the first limb of Answer in Alto, and of the second limb of Subject in First Treble	B♭ minor
"	74 (2)—75	Fragment of the second limb of Subject in Alto. Conclusion, Tierce de Picardie	B♭ major

SUMMARY.

Exposition: Bars 1——17.	Stretti: Two (complete).
Counter-exposition: None.	Coda: Bars 72——75.
Counter-subject: None.	Pedal: None.
Episodes: Three.	

FUGUE XXII.

REMARKS.

(1.) This Fugue is in five parts. It has a "tonal" Answer, and would be styled a "tonal" Fugue. The alterations in the Answer, for the sake of tonality, are made from the first note to the second, and from the second note to the third.

(2.) In the Codetta (bars (5——11 (^{3}) the Second Treble imitates the First Treble at the fourth below, at the distance of a minim.

(3.) The concluding note of the Theme is on five occasions altered to major instead of remaining minor, two of these instances occurring in the Exposition. (Compare Fugue, No. VI.).

(4.) The Episodes are built upon the second limb of the Subject, treated sometimes by similar and sometimes by contrary motion.

(5.) Three things are noticeable in the Stretti: (1) they are both made in a descending direction; (2) the closest Stretto is reserved for the last; (3) though not built upon a Pedal, both of them are exceedingly fine.

PRELUDE XXIII.

SUMMARY.

Bars 1—6, PERIOD I. (ending with a Perfect Cadence in the key of the Dominant).

Bars 6—10 (^{3}), PERIOD II. (ending with a Perfect Cadence in the key of the Submediant).

Bars 10—15, PERIOD III. (ending with a Perfect Cadence in the key of the Tonic).

Bars 15—19, PERIOD IV. CODA.

Bars 1—3 ($\frac{1}{4}$), Tonic Pedal.

Bars 17, 18 ($\frac{1}{4}$), Dominant Pedal.

REMARKS.

This Prelude is constructed upon the figures which appear in bar 1, that in the Treble being used most frequently.

In bar 6 the figures of bar 1 are reproduced in the key of the Dominant, but the Treble of the former becomes the Bass of the latter, and *vice versâ*.

Bar 12 is in a descending Sequence with bar 11.

The following list furnishes every instance of the Principal Theme used in its inverted form: —

> (1) In the Bass part at bar 12.
>
> (2) In the Treble part at bar 15.
>
> (3) In the Treble part at bar 16.
>
> (4) In the Tenor part at bar 17.
>
> (5) In the Treble part at bar 18.
>
> (6) In the Alto part at bar 18.

PRELUDE XXIII.
B MAJOR.
SHOWING THE MELODIC FEATURES AND PHRASING.

Allegretto grazioso, e sempre legato. ♩ = 80.

PERIOD I. B Major, establishing the key. From here it works away for contrast to the key of the Dominant. PERIOD II. From here it works to the Relative Minor and confirms it by a Perfect Cadence. PERIOD III. Descending Sequence. Here it turns homewards to the Tonic. CODA. PERIOD IV. *Imitation of Tenor* (bar 17). Here it strengthens the Dominant Pedal, and clenches the Tonic **key.**

(78)

FUGUE XXIII. (B MAJOR).

IN FOUR PARTS.

Andante con espress. ♩ = 63.

ANALYSIS.

ENUNCIATION SECTION.

Bars			KEYS.
Bars	1 (-1) — 3 (1)	Subject in Tenor	**B**
"	3 (-1) — 5 (1)	Tonal Answer in Alto	**F♯**
"	3 (-2) — 4 (4)	Counter-subject in Tenor.	
"	5 (-1) — 7 (½)	Subject in Treble. Counter-subject in Alto	**B**
"	7 (-1) — 9	Answer in Bass. Counter-subject in Treble	**F♯**
"	9 — 11	Codetta formed to a limited extent from the first part of the Counter-subject.	
"	11 (-3) — 13 (3)	Subject in Tenor	**B**

MODULATORY SECTION.

"	13 — 16	Episode I., modulating from B to F♯.	
"	16 (-1) — 17 (3)	Subject in Alto and Close in F♯ (Dominant)	**F♯**
"	18 (-1) — 20 (1)	Subject by Inversion in Treble	**F♯**
"	20 (-1) — 22 (2)	Answer by Inversion in Alto	**F♯**
"	21 (-3) — 23 (3)	Subject in Bass	**B**
"	24 (-1) — 26 (1)	Answer in Tenor and Close in C♯ minor	**C♯ minor**
"	26 — 29	Episode II., modulating from C♯ minor to B major.	

RECAPITULATORY SECTION.

"	29 (-1) — 31 (½)	Subject in Alto	**B**
"	31 (-1) — 33	Answer in Treble. Counter-subject in Alto	**F♯**
"	33 — 34	Coda	**B**
"	33 (-3) — 34	Reminiscences of first few notes of Counter-subject in Tenor	**B**

SUMMARY.

Exposition : Bars 1 (-1) — 9 (1).
Counter-exposition : None.
Episodes : Two.
Stretti : None.
Pedal : None.
Coda : Bars 33 — 34.

REMARKS.

(1.) This Fugue has a "tonal" Answer, and would be called a "tonal" Fugue. The alteration in the Answer, for the sake of tonality, is made from the first to the second and from the fifth to the sixth notes.

(2.) After the Exposition the Counter-subject is only used once in its entirety, and that near the end of the movement (bars 31 (2) — 33). On two occasions (bar **12** in the Alto and bar **17** in the Treble) its second half only is used. On other occasions it is absent.

(3.) The Episodes are constructed upon the first part of the Counter-subject, though only to a limited extent. At bars 14 — 15 its first limb appears in the Tenor, and at 26 — 27 it appears in the Bass.

In the Coda there occurs a reminiscence of the last part of the Counter-subject in the Treble and of the first part in the Tenor (bar 33).

PRELUDE XXIV.

SUMMARY.

Bars 1—17, PERIOD I. (ending with a Half Cadence in the key of the Tonic).

Bars 16 (^{2}), 17, SHORT CODA.

Bars 18—47, PERIOD II. (working by Sequences mainly through various keys, and finally ending with Tierce de Picardie).

Bars 46 (^{3}), 47, SHORT CODA. (Compare bars 16 and 17).

REMARKS.

In the construction of this Prelude, the first half (PERIOD I.) consists of Imitations in the two upper parts upon a short Theme, accompanied by a moving Bass.

In the second half the structure is much the same, but the figure proposed for Imitation is still shorter, quavers being employed instead of crotchets.

Bars 28—31 are Imitations of the Phrase which first appears in bars 26, 27.

Both Periods are capable of subdivision: Period I. at bars 7 (^{3}), 12 (^{1}), and 16 (^{1}); Period II. at bars 27 (^{3}), 31 (^{3}), and 46 (^{3}).

PRELUDE XXIV.

B MINOR.

SHOWING THE STRUCTURE.

PRELUDE XXIV.

Dominant, then back to B Minor, with close there. Coda, with Half close on the Dominant.

Period II. Sequence (descending). F# Minor. It now touches upon E Minor, D Major, . . . then F#. its

Dominant Minor; and further confirms this key. Then it passes to

E Minor, D Major, ... B Minor . (Sequence).

Then to A Major, ... E Minor, . . B Minor, gradually strengthening the

impression of the original key up to the conclusion. Coda.

Tonic Pedal.

FUGUE XXIV. (B MINOR).

IN FOUR PARTS.

ANALYSIS.

ENUNCIATION SECTION.

<table>
<tr><td>Bars</td><td>1 (-1) ___ 4 (¾)</td><td>Subject in Alto ... ...</td><td>B</td></tr>
<tr><td>"</td><td>4 (-1) ___ 7 (¾)</td><td>Tonal Answer in Tenor, with Counter-subject in Alto ... ...</td><td>F♯ minor</td></tr>
<tr><td>"</td><td>7 ___ 9</td><td>Codetta.</td><td></td></tr>
<tr><td>"</td><td>9 (-1) ___ 12 (¾)</td><td>Subject in Bass. Counter-subject in Tenor ... ...</td><td>B minor</td></tr>
<tr><td>"</td><td>13 ___ 16</td><td>Answer in Treble. Counter-subject in Bass ... ...</td><td>F♯ minor</td></tr>
<tr><td>"</td><td>16 ___ 21</td><td>Episode I., modulating from B minor, through F♯, again to B minor
(observe the fragment of Subject of three notes only in Alto, bar 19).</td><td></td></tr>
<tr><td>"</td><td>21 (-1) ___ 24 (1)</td><td>Subject in Alto. Counter-subject in Treble... ... ...</td><td>B minor</td></tr>
</table>

MODULATORY SECTION.

<table>
<tr><td>"</td><td>24 ___ 30</td><td>Episode II., modulating from F♯ minor through B to E minor (observe
the fragment of Answer of three notes only in Tenor, bar 28).</td><td></td></tr>
<tr><td>"</td><td>30 (-1) ___ 33</td><td>Subject in Tenor. Counter-subject slightly altered in Treble ... ...</td><td>E minor</td></tr>
<tr><td>"</td><td>34 (-1) ___ 35 (1)</td><td>Stretto I. (incomplete), Subject in Alto. Counter-subject absent ...</td><td>F♯ minor</td></tr>
<tr><td>"</td><td>35 (-1) ___ 36 (2)</td><td>Subject in Treble ... ...</td><td>B minor</td></tr>
<tr><td>"</td><td>38 (-1) ___ 41 (¾)</td><td>Subject in Bass. Counter-subject in Treble ... ...</td><td>B minor</td></tr>
<tr><td>"</td><td>41 (-1) ___ 42 (1)</td><td>Subject (first part) in Treble ... ...</td><td>B minor</td></tr>
<tr><td>"</td><td>42 (-1) ___ 43 (1)</td><td>Subject (first part) in Alto ... ...</td><td>E minor</td></tr>
<tr><td>"</td><td>43 ___ 44</td><td>Subject (first part) in Bass ... ...</td><td>A major</td></tr>
<tr><td>"</td><td>44 (-1) ___ 46 (3)</td><td>Subject in Tenor. Part of Counter-subject in Alto</td><td>D major</td></tr>
<tr><td>"</td><td>47 (-3) ___ 50 (3)</td><td>Answer in Bass. Counter-subject in Treble ... ...</td><td>D major</td></tr>
<tr><td>"</td><td>50 ___ 53 (3)</td><td>Episode III., modulating from D to F♯ minor.</td><td></td></tr>
<tr><td>"</td><td>53 (-3) ___ 56 (3)</td><td>Subject in Tenor. Counter-subject in Treble ... ...</td><td>F♯ minor</td></tr>
<tr><td>"</td><td>57 (-3) ___ 60 (3)</td><td>Subject in Bass. Counter-subject in Treble ... ...</td><td>E major</td></tr>
<tr><td>"</td><td>60 (-3) ___ 63 (4)</td><td>Subject in Tenor. Counter-subject absent ... ...</td><td>B minor</td></tr>
<tr><td>"</td><td>64 ___ 69</td><td>Episode IV., modulating from F♯ minor to B minor.</td><td></td></tr>
<tr><td>"</td><td>69 (-1) ___ 70 (2)</td><td>Subject (first part) in Tenor ... ...</td><td>B minor</td></tr>
<tr><td>"</td><td>70 (-1) ___ 72 (4)</td><td>Stretto III. (incomplete), Subject in Bass. Counter-subject in Treble ...</td><td>E minor</td></tr>
</table>

Stretto II. (complete) — bracketing bars 41–46.

RECAPITULATORY SECTION

<table>
<tr><td>"</td><td>73 ___ 76</td><td>Coda ... ...</td><td>B minor</td></tr>
<tr><td>"</td><td>74 ___ 75 (¾)</td><td>Dominant Pedal.</td><td></td></tr>
<tr><td>"</td><td>74 (-1) ___ 75 (1)</td><td>Subject in Alto. Conclusion, Tierce de Picardie ... ...</td><td>B major</td></tr>
</table>

SUMMARY.

Exposition : Bars 1 ___ 16.
Counter-exposition : None.
Episodes : Four.
Stretti : One, complete. Two, incomplete.
Dominant Pedal : Bars 74 ___ 75 (¾).
Coda : Bars 73 ___ 76.

FUGUE XXIV.

REMARKS.

(1.) This Fugue has a "tonal" Answer, and would be called a "tonal" Fugue. The alteration in the Answer, for the sake of tonality, is made at the second and fifth notes.

(2.) Episode I. for two bars is formed upon the last eight notes of the Counter-subject. From bar 17 to 20 the Bass moves in a descending sequence with a figure four quavers in length, and upon it appear canonical imitations (based on an entirely new figure) between the Treble and Tenor.

Episode II. is formed from the same material as Episode I., but at bars 28——29 the figure of the Bass is altered.

Episode III., the same material is used as in the preceding Episodes, but the canonical imitations are here omitted.

Episode IV. is much the same as Episodes I. and II. in construction. The canonical work is here given to the Treble and Alto.

(3.) Stretti I. and III. are incomplete because all the voices do not take part in them. In the former the Alto and Treble alone take part (bars 34——35), in the latter only the Tenor and Bass (bars 69——70). Stretto II. is complete, all the voices taking part in it (bars 41——46).

Printed and bound in Great Britain by
Caligraving Limited Thetford Norfolk

1/99 (33135)